THE TIMES *management library*

Decision Theory and the Manager

£7-50

Decision Theory and the Manager

Howard Thomas B.Sc., M.Sc., M.B.A., Ph.D.
London Graduate School of Business Studies

 Pitman Publishing

First published 1972

SIR ISAAC PITMAN AND SONS LTD.
Pitman House, Parker Street, Kingsway, London, WC2B 5PB
P.O. Box 46038, Portal Street, Nairobi, Kenya

SIR ISAAC PITMAN (AUST.) PTY. LTD.
Pitman House, 158 Bouverie Street, Carlton, Victoria 3053, Australia

PITMAN PUBLISHING COMPANY S.A. LTD.
P.O. Box 11231, Johannesburg, S. Africa

PITMAN PUBLISHING CORPORATION
6 East 43rd Street, New York, N.Y. 10017, U.S.A.

SIR ISAAC PITMAN (CANADA) LTD.
495 Wellington Street West, Toronto 135, Canada

THE COPP CLARK PUBLISHING COMPANY
517 Wellington Street West, Toronto 135, Canada

©
Howard Thomas
1972

ISBN: 0 273 31534 X

Text set in 10/11 pt. Monotype Times New Roman, printed by letterpress, and
bound in Great Britain at The Pitman Press, Bath
G2—(TML 2: 51)

To Dorothy and Jonathan

Preface

The post second World War phenomenon in business management has been the rapid expansion of computer facilities and departments of management science, operations research, systems analysis and so on within firms. To many managers the workings of computers and O.R. models are often incomprehensible and specialists in management science areas sometimes find it difficult to implement their suggestions because of management scepticism.

The development of graduate business schools in the U.K. will undoubtedly increase the willingness of British managers to follow American counterparts and learn about and implement the findings of O.R. techniques. It is the manager's function to make decisions and in that task he needs all the help he can get. Some of the most difficult problems which regularly confront managers are investment decisions. Should new production facilities be built? Should new products be introduced? In nearly all cases the basis of the difficulty is the uncertainty which is an inherent part of such problems.

It is the dual aim of this book to present a framework for the logical analysis of decision problems and to show how this framework can be applied to a number of realistic business situations. It is the author's firm belief that the decision analysis framework should primarily be used as a means of formulating the essential elements and difficulties in any given decision problem. If a decision-maker learns to communicate in terms of this framework with an O.R. specialist then the solution of his decision problems can be attacked much more meaningfully by that specialist.

The book is itself divided into three parts. Part I covers the basic foundations of the methodology of decision analysis. Part II shows how the techniques of decision analysis may be used to solve decision problems by means of illustration through a number of short case studies. Part III discusses the hurdles that have to be scaled in implementing decision analysis methods in a business context.

In writing a book on this subject there are a number of people whose guidance and help has been valuable. Professor H. V. Roberts of Chicago who first nurtured my interest in decision theory and Professor Howard Raiffa through his sheer good-naturedness and enthusiasm for decision theory are the two individuals to whom I owe the greatest debt.

I wish also to thank my father Elwyn Thomas who read this book from the viewpoint of the potential reader and my wife and son for their cheerfulness and guidance throughout this project. In addition, my wife skilfully typed and edited the final manuscript.

Finally, I wish to acknowledge the support of two excellent departmental heads, Professor N. C. Hunt of the Department of Business Studies, University of Edinburgh, and Professor P. G. Moore of the London Graduate School of Business Studies.

To John Hudson of Pitman and his predecessor Malcolm Stern I award the prizes for patience in ironing out difficulties and tact in persuading me to finish a book first mooted in 1968.

The index was kindly prepared by Mr. K. G. B. Bakewell.

Chesham, 1972   H.T.

Contents

ix

Part III: Implementation of Decision-analysis Techniques

PART I

Basic Foundations of Decision-theory Analysis

1 *Basic Ideas of Probability Theory and Uncertainty*

Probability theory is that branch of statistical methods which deals with problems of uncertainty. Whilst the basic ideas of probability are familiar from everyday experience there is a need to define the basic concepts of probability precisely. We talk of rain being probable on a particular day and speculate about the improbability of winning the £50,000 prize in the Premium Bonds draw. Business executives in their day-to-day activities make statements such as "it is likely that the demand for our products will fall" or "even if we raise the price of our product we are very likely to keep all of our customers". Each of these statements on its own has meaning for the individual or business executive but not necessarily for a third person. The third person may discern a difference between "possible" and "probable" and feel that the business executive is using a rough scale of measurement, e.g. unlikely, likely or very likely, to express his degree of belief in the likelihood of its occurrence. Probability theory tries to develop this intuitive idea of a rough qualitative scale of measurement in order to obtain a numerical scale of measurement which will express the individual's assessments of the likelihood of occurrence of, say, rain or a downturn in demand for a product.

In our study of decision theory and decision trees in the next two chapters we shall see that probabilistic methods are one of the key elements in the analysis of decisions under uncertainty. As our main interest is to analyse business decisions under uncertainty we should first of all discuss what we mean by uncertainty and indicate how it is likely to affect typical business decisions and, particularly, investment decisions. This discussion is a necessary prerequisite for understanding why the systematic analysis of business decisions requires a knowledge of probability theory and probabilistic methods.

3

UNCERTAINTY

Uncertainty exists if a process can lead to *several* possible outcomes. For example, an investment decision by a manager in new plant or equipment will lead to some return on investment over future years of the firm's operations. However, the exact rate of return is uncertain but will probably be within the outcome band −5 to +25 per cent, say. This means that the investment decision can lead to several probable rates of return, though which of these will occur is not known exactly.

There are two main ways in which the effects of uncertainty on decision problems can be analysed. First, we can look at the spectrum of uncertain elements which affect the decision problem. Second, we can look at the process of uncertainty itself and see whether it can be described in statistical terms.

Let us consider investment-decision problems which are made in the face of uncertainty and structure our discussion around the effects of uncertainty on investment decision.

Uncertainties in the real world range across a wide spectrum. Not all of them affect individual investment decisions but it is useful to outline the potentially uncertain elements in a general investment-decision situation. Investment decisions are made by firms in an environment of political uncertainty. For example, successive Labour and Conservative governments have changed the scope and nature of investment incentives and grants for firms locating new plants in development areas. Clearly, no rational decision-maker should take these incentives into account in deciding where to locate a new plant because the life of a government of a particular philosophy, say five to seven years on average, is often considerably less than the time horizon over which the return on investment for the new plant should be assessed. Thus, too frequent changes in tax policies and investment incentives make investment decision-making a complex task and help to create an environment of uncertainty in which business planning is made more difficult.

A phenomenon which increasingly affects industry in its investment decision-making is the effect of technological change. Technological change affects the production possibilities open to the firm, renders some existing products obsolescent—e.g. valves were quickly made obsolescent with the advent of the transistor—changes and shifts the market for new and existing products and can threaten the whole future existence of the firm. Often firms are forced to try and forecast potential future technological developments in order to make sense of the future prospects of certain investment options at present open to them. Nowadays, expensive research on valve technology would clearly not produce an adequate payoff because of the rapid growth of microelectronic devices like the transistor.

To a large extent political and technological uncertainties are common externalities to firms in a given industry. Firms face internal uncertainties caused by their interaction with other firms in the same industry. For example, if a firm is about to launch a new product it is probably uncertain about the reactions to the product of other competitors in the industry. These competitors may introduce alternative products or intensively market, perhaps through a cut-throat pricing policy, some of their own existing competitive, but technically inferior, instruments. Quite apart from uncertainties about competitors' reactions, the firm, in an investment-decision situation may be faced with the problem of resolving uncertainties about the estimation of the investment costs and cash flows which might be expected to accrue as a result of undertaking the investment project over some future planning period.

Now that we have evaluated some of the component elements, external and internal, of uncertainty in an investment-decision problem for a firm, we should recognize that investment decisions can be viewed in terms of the particular nature of the problem and the degree to which the decision-maker can reduce the impact of uncertainty on his investment decision. There is a class of investment decisions which can be regarded as once-and-for-all decisions. For example, the introduction of a technically sophisticated aero engine may put great strains on a company's resources, yet it knows that a failure to capitalize on this opportunity must make it unlikely that it will be strong enough to exploit others. The decision is a once-and-for-all decision because, strategically, the launch has to be done now despite all the uncertainties about demand, costs of development and sheer technical feasibility.

In other circumstances decision-makers may consciously view a particular investment decision as being one element of a series of decisions. Conglomerate companies make investment decisions which are unique but try to achieve a balance between risky and relatively safe projects, so that it is reasonable to regard the risk overall as being small, particularly if successive decisions are uncorrelated.

Another strategy which a decision-maker may adopt in order to reduce uncertainty is to choose a sequential pattern for arriving at a decision. In research and development decision-making, research managers often postpone decisions to start programmes of research in new technical areas until they have had the opportunity to do some additional research and obtain further information about the feasibility of research in that technical area. Such additional research and information is obtained at extra cost and delays the start of the research. There is, therefore, inevitably a trade-off between the reduction of uncertainty about the technical area and the delay in starting the research. This trade-off needs to be balanced finely if we are to avoid the possibility of procrastination on the part of decision-makers and research and development managers.

It is possible also for a decision-maker who makes the same decision repetitively over a period of time to treat the decision process as a stable statistical process. This will allow statistical techniques to be applied to such repetitive decision processes as, for example, inventory-control decisions in production management.

Uncertainty, therefore, is present in all investment-decision problems. Uncertainties about the final outcomes or the factors such as cost, etc., which make up the decision problem have to be resolved in some way. One natural way is to try to express the degree of uncertainty in decision problems in terms of a common vocabulary and scale of measurement. Instead of rough qualitative statements of the type "likely", "probable" and "unlikely", we need a numerical scale of measurement for the probability or odds of, say, a high rate of return in an investment-decision problem.

THE MEANING OF PROBABILITY

The quantitative approach to uncertainty, as we have seen, requires that we try to assess the content of statements about uncertainty on a numerical scale. We must make explicit what decision-makers mean by weighing the odds or taking calculated risks. We start by asserting that the greatest degree of probability which any event can have is obviously "certainty". An example of a certain event is that you will die some day. Similarly, we define the lowest degree of probability which any event can have as "impossibility". There can be no event which is less likely to occur than an event which is impossible. In most cases the extremes of "certainty" or "impossibility" on the probability scale are never likely to be attained. Most events for which we will require probability assessments lie somewhere between "certainty" and "impossibility". We arbitrarily assign to the event "certainty" a probability of 1·0 and to the event "impossibility" a probability of 0·0.

Several different methods of measuring probabilities have been suggested. All of them, however, follow the probability scale of measurement ranging from 0·0 to 1·0. Each of these different methods represents a different conceptual position about the meaning of probability. The three methods we shall consider are based on the concepts of *a priori probability*, *relative frequency* and *subjective probability*.

A priori Probability

The *a priori* concept of probability was developed from observations of games of chance. For example, if we toss a coin it can fall either "head" or "tail". If the coin is unbiased, both are equally likely. We can, therefore, say that the probability of head $= \frac{1}{2}$ (if we neglect the occurrence of the extremely unlikely outcome that the coin lands on its edge). This intuitive discussion leads to the formal definition for the probability of some event, E.

$$\text{Probability of } E = \frac{\text{Number of outcomes favourable to occurrence of } E}{\text{Total number of possible outcomes}}$$

To illustrate quickly that this definition makes sense, let us apply it to the coin-tossing experiment to find the probability of the event "head" in one toss of a coin. There are two possible outcomes, head or tail, which are equally likely, and, therefore, the probability of head $= \frac{1}{2}$.

This rule can also be applied to show quite simply that the probability of a specified number thrown on one throw of a die is $\frac{1}{6}$.

This concept of probability, based on equally likely outcomes, has little application as a means of measuring probabilities in situations other than games of chance. Consider the probability assessment for the event that a male British subject, age 25, will die within the next year. There are only two possible occurrences, namely that he will still be alive at the end of the year or that he will die during the year. Intuitively, the probability of death is much smaller than the probability of staying alive though the exact values could only be obtained from statistical mortality data. The crucial point to note, however, is that the two possible outcomes do *not* have equal likelihoods of happening, and so the *a priori* concept of probability cannot be used to give the probabilities of life and death.

The Relative Frequency Concept of Probability

A much more useful concept of probability, in practical terms, can be seen in terms of the example of the probability of survival or death of a male individual aged 25 in a one-year period. It was suggested that values for these probabilities could be obtained from mortality data. Actuaries collect simple information on the number of deaths that occur within a cohort sample of, say, 100,000 men aged 25 during a one-year period. The relative frequency or probability of death is given as the number of deaths divided by the total sample at risk, i.e. 100,000 men in the case we have illustrated. The principle on which the relative-frequency concept is based is that information obtained from some experiment or from the process itself enables us to identify the probability of some event within the process, i.e. if we are studying the mortality of individuals of all ages in given time periods we try to observe from the sample at our disposal the relative frequencies with which deaths occur for each age-band and so obtain probabilities of death and survival in terms of the relative-frequency concept.

The relative-frequency concept of probability, therefore, depends heavily upon the availability of objective information about the event whose probability we require to find. In many production problems, say in process control, we can observe the number of defective items produced by the production process at periodic intervals and determine whether or not the process is in control by looking for changes in the probability of obtaining a defective item from the process. If this probability increases significantly it is reasonable to suppose that some characteristics of the process have altered and, therefore, that the process may be out of control. In many other business problems it is very difficult to observe the statistical properties of the process in a meaningful way. Take for example a firm launching a new product. It cannot observe the process of launching this new product ten or say twenty times, neither can it make the case very often that other new product launches by the firm will help it to assess objectively the probability of success of the current new product launch. Whilst the marketing manager cannot get an objective assessment of the probability of a successful launch, he nevertheless has his own views about the product and its likely success. These introspective feelings and judgements lead us to the third of our concepts of probability, i.e. subjective probability, as a reflection of the individual's subjective belief in the occurrence of some particular event.

Subjective Probability

A marketing manager launching a new product obviously has subjective feelings about the likely success of the product even if he is unable to draw upon objective information to make his case seem more conclusive. It is useful, therefore, to develop a concept of probability around an individual decision-maker's degrees of belief in some event particularly in business situations, such as the marketing of new products, in which objective information is hard to come by and uncertainty is great.

8

We define the subjective probability of an event as an assessment of the individual decision-maker's current degree of belief about the occurrence of that event. The marketing manager may assign a probability of 0·6 to the event "success" of the new product. This means that a probability of 0·4 must be assigned to the event "failure" if the probability assessments are to be consistent. In other words the product will either be a success or a failure: nothing else can happen. Therefore, in terms of our numerical probability scale, the probability of success and the probability of failure must sum to 1.

We shall use the subjective-probability concept very often in the analysis of decision problems in this book. In order to do this we must know how to obtain probability assessments from decision-makers which are consistent and satisfactory in their representation of the decision-maker's degrees of belief. We shall tackle this problem more fully in a later section of this chapter once the reader has been more thoroughly versed in other dimensions of probability theory.

Properties of a Probability Measure

We note here briefly what we understand by a numerical measure of probability. First, given a set of possible events which make up the only possible outcomes in a particular situation, we can say that the probability of any event must be a number between 0 and 1, i.e. it must range somewhere between the extremes of "impossibility" and "certainty". Second, the sum of probabilities of all the events in that particular situation must add up to 1, i.e. certainty.

Let us just make this quite clear by means of an example. Suppose that a firm requires to find out what the demand for its product is likely to be. It asks a market-research firm to ascertain whether the demand for its products will be *high*, *medium* or *low* and to assign probabilities to the attainment of *high*, *medium* and *low* demand levels (where we leave aside definitional problems of what we mean by high, medium or low demand). The only possible events in this probability assessment situation are *high*, *medium* or *low* demand. Therefore, the probabilities of each must be numbers between 0 and 1 and the sum of the probabilities of *high*, *medium* and *low* demand must be 1.

Let us check that the market-research firm has produced reasonable probability assessments for each of the sales levels. Suppose that it finds that the probability of high demand, $P(H)$, is 0·4, the probability of medium demand, $P(M)$, is 0·5 and $P(L)$, the probability of low demand, is 0·1.

These probability assessments certainly meet both of our conditions for a probability measure. Each of $P(H)$, $P(M)$ and $P(L)$ lies between 0 and 1 numerically and the sum $P(H) + P(M) + P(L) = 1$, i.e. no other demand levels than high, medium or low can occur.

Probability and Uncertainty

At this stage of the chapter we should try to establish in our minds the link between the concepts of probability and uncertainty. We have discussed a number of alternative ways of conceptualizing probability and have indicated that uncertainty is a subjective quantity, with definable elements, which pervades most business decision problems.

It is roughly true to say that, once the probability of occurrence of some event of interest is assessed, the magnitude of uncertainty is defined. To illustrate this consider three different assessments for the probability of rain tomorrow. Mr A assigns a probability of 0·05, Mr B assigns a probability of 0·5, whilst Mr C assigns a probability of 0·95. Mr A and Mr C judge that rain is very unlikely and very likely to occur respectively. In their minds the degree of uncertainty attached to the event "rain tomorrow" is very small. Mr B on the other hand assesses a 50/50 chance to rain and this assessment indicates that his degree of uncertainty is at its maximum value, because rain or fine weather are equally likely events. It follows from this intuitive discussion that when the probability of any event (it doesn't have to be rain) is approximately $\frac{1}{2}$, uncertainty about that event is greatest. This uncertainty decreases as the probability either falls below or increases above the value $\frac{1}{2}$.

The probability concept therefore gives us an indication of the quantitative magnitude of uncertainty about some event once a probability assessment for the occurrence of the event has been made.

We need now to develop our understanding about the nature of probability to gain an appreciation of how we obtain probability values for compound events. For example, given that we have probability assessments for high and medium sales as being 0·4 and 0·5 respectively (from the earlier example), how do we obtain the probability of the compound event, "either high or medium sales". Clearly, in this simple case the probability required is $0·4 + 0·5 = 0·9$.

Probabilities of Compound Events or Rules of Probability

We have discussed already how to obtain probability values for simple events, e.g. the probability of "head" on one toss of a coin is $\frac{1}{2}$. Also, the probability of the compound event "either head or tail" is $\frac{1}{2} + \frac{1}{2} = 1$.

Suppose that we are now asked to find the probability of getting three heads if we toss a coin three times. We exhibit the logic of this coin-tossing experiment in Table 1.1.

TABLE 1.1

Tree Diagram for Three Trials of a Coin-tossing Experiment

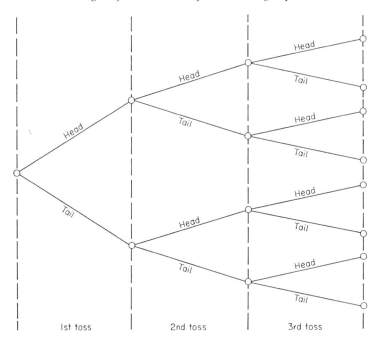

On the first toss of the coin either a head or a tail can happen. Again, given we obtain a head on the first toss we could get a head or a tail on the second toss and so on through the diagram, e.g. given a head on the first toss and a head on the second toss, there is a possibility of obtaining a head or a tail on the third toss. The tree diagram thus shows that there are eight possible outcomes of the experiment as exhibited by the final tips of the tree. We can equally well see quite easily that the event "three heads" is one of the final eight outcomes and we can evaluate its probability as being $\frac{1}{8}$, i.e. the ratio of the number of outcomes favourable to the event three "heads" to the total number of outcomes (8) at the tips of the tree.

11

From these few simple examples we can intuitively develop a number of rules for obtaining probabilities of compound events and these rules should, therefore, be viewed as being merely formalizations of common-sense reasoning about probabilities.

We need first of all to introduce a little bit of mathematical notation in order to express our probability rules as concisely as possible. Our interest is in the notion of compound events. We can think of a compound event in terms of an experiment which can give rise to a series of possible events A_1, A_2, A_3, etc. It is quite possible in such cases for the probabilities of, say, A_1 and A_2 to overlap.

Consider, for example, an experiment in which we throw a die once. Let A_1 be the event "the score is less than or equal to three" and A_2 be the event "the score is an odd number". We know that there are six possible outcomes when a die is thrown, i.e. 1, 2, 3, 4, 5 or 6. The event A_1 therefore consists of the outcomes 1, 2, and 3, i.e. (1, 2, 3) whereas A_2 consists of the outcomes 1, 3, and 5, i.e. (1, 3, 5). Now the event "A_1 and A_2 happen together" denoted by (A_1A_2) consists of the outcomes 1 and 3, i.e. (1, 3) and the event "either A_1 happens or A_2 happens or both happen" denoted by $(A_1 + A_2)$ consists of the outcomes 1, 2, 3 and 5, i.e. (1, 2, 3, 5). We can easily determine probability values for the events (A_1A_2) and $(A_1 + A_2)$. $P(A_1A_2)$, the probability of the event (A_1A_2) is $\frac{2}{6} = \frac{1}{3}$, i.e. it is the ratio of the number of outcomes favourable to the event (A_1A_2), i.e. 2, to the total number of outcomes, i.e. 6. Similarly, $P(A_1 + A_2) = \frac{4}{6} = \frac{2}{3}$.

With the notational preliminaries explained and developed, we can now baldly present the probability rules. First, the addition rule for probabilities.

Addition Rule for Probabilities

Suppose A_1 and A_2 are two events associated with some experiment (such as throwing dice).
Then

$$P(A_1 + A_2) = P(A_1) + P(A_2) - P(A_1A_2)$$

The intuitive justification for this rule is illustrated in Table 1.2. Suppose that we are considering the dice-throwing experiment discussed earlier. There are six possible outcomes denoted by dots in the diagram and the set of outcomes corresponding to A_1 and to A_2 are encircled.

Since the event (A_1A_2) occurs we cannot calculate $P(A_1 + A_2)$ as being the sum of $P(A_1)$ and $P(A_2)$. This is clear from the diagram because the probability corresponding to $A_1 + A_2$ is $\dfrac{4}{6}$ which is not the same as $P(A_1) + P(A_2)$, i.e. 1, because A_1 and A_2 overlap, i.e. (A_1A_2) has a probability of $\frac{2}{6} = \frac{1}{3}$ which must be subtracted from 1 to give the correct value for $P(A_1 + A_2)$.

TABLE 1.2

Diagrammatic Representation of Dice-throwing Experiment

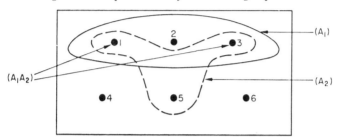

In our rule therefore, $P(A_1) = \frac{1}{2}$, $P(A_2) = \frac{1}{2}$, $P(A_1A_2) = \frac{1}{3}$, giving
$$P(A_1 + A_2) = P(A_1) + P(A_2) - P(A_1A_2)$$
$$= \tfrac{1}{2} + \tfrac{1}{2} - \tfrac{1}{3} = \tfrac{2}{3}$$

On the other hand, if A_1 and A_2 cannot happen together, i.e. event (A_1A_2) has no elements,
$$P(A_1 + A_2) = P(A_1) + P(A_2)$$

Suppose, for example, that we redefine our event A_2. Let A_2 be "a score of 5 or 6" and A_1 still be "a score less than or equal to 3" on one throw of a dice. In this case (A_1A_2) has no elements and
$$P(A_1 + A_2) = P(A_1) + P(A_2)$$
$$= \tfrac{1}{2} + \tfrac{1}{3} = \tfrac{5}{6}$$

Second, the next rule we shall formally consider is the multiplication rule for probabilities.

Multiplication Rule for Probabilities

The purpose of this rule is to obtain an expression for the probability of the event (A_1A_2) in terms of the probabilities of single events. In order to do so it is necessary to introduce the concept of conditional probability. This concept can best be understood in terms of an example. Suppose that a consumer goes into an electric

13

shop to buy an electric light bulb and he is offered a choice of two types, A and B, at similar prices. Suppose that the dealer knows that 0·83 of all type-A bulbs are perfect and that 0·65 of type-B bulbs are perfect. Therefore, if the consumer buys a type-A bulb, the probability he will purchase a good bulb is 0·83. This means that the probability of him getting a good bulb *conditional* on its being type A is 0·83. Similarly, his *conditional* probability of getting a good bulb if it is of type B is only 0·65. We write this P(good bulb/type B) $= 0.65$, i.e. the probability of a good bulb given type B is 0·65.

Now that we have illustrated the meaning of a conditional probability we can present the multiplication rule for probabilities. The rule states that the probability that "A_1 and A_2 happen together" is the product of the conditional probability of A_2 given A_1 and the probability of A_1, i.e.

$$P(A_1A_2) = P(A_2/A_1) \times P(A_1)$$

Let us consider an example to illustrate this rule:

EXAMPLE
An urn contains two black and four white balls. Suppose we draw two at random without replacement (i.e. we do not replace any ball after picking it), then what is the probability that both balls are white?

Let A_1 be the event "first ball is white".
Let A_2 be the event "second ball is white".

Now (A_1A_2) denotes the event "both balls are white".
From the rule $P(A_1A_2) = P(A_2/A_1) \times P(A_1)$

    (i) the probability $P(A_1)$ that the first ball is white $= \frac{4}{6}$;
    (ii) the probability $P(A_2/A_1)$ that the second ball is white given that the first ball is white $= \frac{3}{5}$.

Therefore, $P(A_1A_2) = \frac{4}{6} \times \frac{3}{5} = \frac{2}{5}$

We could easily solve this example in terms of the versatile tree diagram first exhibited in Table 1.1. Table 1.3 shows the tree diagram for this example.

From the tree diagram we can see several things. First, the probability that both balls are white is given by the lower branch of the tree and the required probability is given by the product of the probability that the first ball is white ($\frac{2}{3}$, figure in brackets) and the conditional probability that the second ball is white given that the first is white, i.e. $\frac{2}{3}$. Second, that the four branches of the tree on the second draw give the values of the probabilities of second ball black given first black, second ball white given first black, second

14

ball black given first white and second ball white given first white as $\frac{1}{5}$, $\frac{4}{5}$, $\frac{2}{5}$ and $\frac{3}{5}$ respectively.

TABLE 1.3

Tree Diagram for Balls-in-urn Experiment

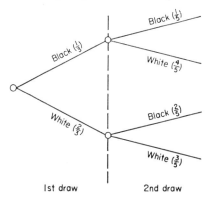

1st draw   2nd draw

There is a special case of the multiplication rule which is useful in practical probability assessment. Suppose now that the probability that the event A_2 occurs is the same whether or not A_1 has occurred, i.e.

$$P(A_2/A_1) = P(A_2)$$

This means that A_1 and A_2 are *statistically* independent events and the form of the multiplication rule for this special case becomes $P(A_1A_2) = P(A_2) \times P(A_1)$.

We return to the balls in the urn example in order to show how this case differs from the general form of the multiplication rule. Suppose that the urn still contains two black and four white balls and that we pick two balls at random. However, the conditions of the experiment have been changed so that we must now replace the balls after we have picked them. If we still let (A_1A_2) be the event that "both balls are white" and (A_1) and (A_2) be the simple events "first white" and "second white" respectively, we can determine the probability of (A_1A_2) as follows:

    (i) the probability (A_1) is still $\frac{4}{6} = \frac{2}{3}$;

    (ii) the probability (A_2/A_1) is identical to the probability of (A_2), i.e. $\frac{2}{3}$, because the event A_2 is now *independent* of A_1. This is a result directly of the experimental condition that the ball selected should be *replaced* after it has been picked out.

    (iii) Therefore $P(A_1A_2) = P(A_1)P(A_2/A_1) = P(A_1)P(A_2)$

$$= \tfrac{2}{3} \times \tfrac{2}{3} = \tfrac{4}{9}$$

15

This can be seen very easily from the tree diagram in Table 1.4.

TABLE 1.4

Tree Diagram for Amended Balls-in-urn Experiment

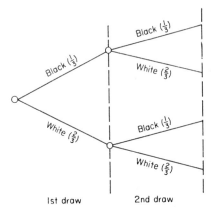

| 1st draw | 2nd draw |

The four branches at the second draw stage show clearly that the probabilities of getting black and white at that stage are completely unaffected by what has happened at the initial stage of drawing the first ball.

From the bottom branch of the amended tree we can see immediately that the probability of both white is $\frac{2}{3} \times \frac{2}{3} = \frac{4}{9}$, i.e. the product of the probabilities along the bottom branch of the tree diagram.

The Relevance of Rules of Probability

At this stage the average reader will probably (subjective probability not assessed!) feel that he would like to sit back and ponder upon the rules of probability. Despite the fact that the examples discussed have had more immediate relevance to students of games of chance the concepts of probability have immediate relevance to business problems. Consider the following example: Imagine that a market-research firm has assigned probabilities of 0·7, 0·2 and 0·1 for *high*, *medium* and *low* sales for a new product, say of a new car in the first year of its launch. The sales staff in the car firm are also interested in the demand for the second year of the car's life. Although they have no specific guidelines or past objective information to help them because the design concept is a relatively new one for the firm, the sales staff nevertheless feel that they are able to assign subjective probabilities for the demand in the second year. They recognize first of all that demand in the second year will depend upon the success of the product in the first year, i.e. on consumer

16

demand in the first year. They agree to draw the structure of the problem in terms of a tree diagram as shown in Table 1.5.

TABLE 1.5

Probability Tree Diagram of Demand for a New Car over a Two-year Period

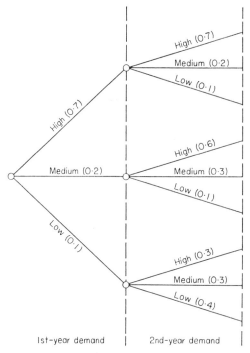

After deliberating amongst themselves they also assigned conditional probabilities of high, medium or low demand given the demand pattern in the first year.

From this tree we can see that the probability of high sales in the first and second years is $0.7 \times 0.7 = 0.49$. Lord Stokes in launching a new car such as the Morris Marina for the British Leyland Motor Corporation would probably not agree with these figures but might agree that a probability analysis of a more realistic type would be valuable for his marketing staff. That more realistic type of probability analysis is the decision-tree analysis which forms the core of the subsequent chapters in this book.

Before we reach the stage of analysing decision problems in a formal and thorough manner a number of other probabilistic ideas have to be discussed. These ideas should appeal to the common sense of the reader; if they do not, then the author's explanation of the ideas, rather than the nature of the ideas themselves, is at fault.

The *ideas* which we hope to establish in succeeding pages are the concepts of a *probability distribution* for some uncertain quantity (such as sales for a new product, or the salary of accountants) and the *expected* value of that uncertain quantity, e.g. expected sales or expected salary. We turn to an intuitive treatment of each of these ideas.

Probability Distributions and Expected Value

A manufacturer may want to know the likely demand for his new car. Uncertainty about that demand exists because the firm cannot possibly have all the facts at its disposal. If it could measure the effectiveness of its newspaper advertisements and the efficiency of its sales force plus a whole host of other uncertain quantities which affect demand, it would be able to predict demand with much greater accuracy. However, no matter how many facts and how much information the firm has at its disposal it has to contend with the variability that is inherent in the process of obtaining the factual information. Repeated measurements of the efficiency of the sales force would not necessarily give the same answers because of the variability in performance of both the methods of measuring efficiency and the salesmen in their day-to-day activities.

Let us now return to the problem of assessing the demand for a new car in the first year of its launch. The sales team meet and feel that the demand for the car will be somewhere between 100,000 and 300,000 cars per year. They then decide to split this range up into chunks of size 25,000 cars and assess the likelihood of occurrence of demand levels within each of these ranges (thousands): 100–125, 125–150, 150–175, 175–200, 200–225, 225–250, 250–275, 275–300. Their assessments are given in Table 1.6.

The set of probability assessments in Table 1.6 together with the associated values of the uncertain quantity, demand level, define the *probability distribution* of the uncertain quantity, demand level. The underlying idea a distribution for demand is that demand is not known with certainty but can take on with given probability certain demand levels within a range of possible demand levels. We can illustrate the probability distribution in terms of a *histogram* and get a better idea and feel for the concept of a distribution. Table 1.7 shows the graphical representation of the probability distribution of demand.

TABLE 1.6

Assessments of Probabilities of Demand Levels for Cars

Demand levels	Probability of demand level
100–125	0·05
125–150	0·05
150–175	0·05
175–200	0·10
200–225	0·10
225–250	0·40
250–275	0·20
275–300	0·05
Total	1·00

This graph or histogram is drawn in the following way: For each possible demand level within the range a block is erected whose height is given by the probability of occurrence of that demand level. A rough smoothed curve has been drawn through the discrete chunks so obtained to give an idea of the form of the distribution. Looking at the graph we can see that the smoothed distribution has two characteristic features. First, an average level of sales somewhere in the range 200–250 and, second, variability or spread about that average. If there were no variability we would expect the distribution to be concentrated around one and only one demand-level band.

TABLE 1.7

Histogram of Probability Distribution for Demand

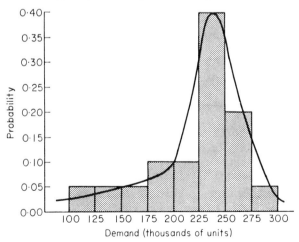

Demand (thousands of units)

19

There are several ways in which we could potentially describe the average tendency of the demand-level distribution. The most commonly used average is arithmetic average. In the context of the probability distribution of an uncertain quantity, such as demand, the analogous concept to the arithmetic average is the *expected value* of that uncertain quantity, demand. This *expected demand* is obtained by taking each possible demand value within the range (for each demand band, assume that the representative value is the mid-point value), multiplying it by the probability of occurrence of that demand value given in Table 1.6 and summing all such values. The calculation is detailed immediately below:

TABLE 1.8

Expected Demand Calculation for Probability Distribution of Demand

Expected demand = $(112\cdot5 \times 0\cdot05) + (137\cdot5 \times 0\cdot05)$
$+ (162\cdot5 \times 0\cdot05) + (187\cdot5 \times 0\cdot1)$
$+ (212\cdot5 \times 0\cdot1) + (237\cdot5 \times 0\cdot4)$
$+ (262\cdot5 \times 0\cdot2) + (287\cdot5 \times 0\cdot05)$
(In words this equation says: sum the possible demand levels weighted by their probabilities of occurrence to get the appropriate expected value.)
$= 5\cdot6 + 6\cdot9 + 8\cdot1 + 18\cdot7 + 21\cdot3 + 95\cdot0 + 52\cdot5$
$+ 14\cdot4$
$= 222\cdot5$ thousand units

The expected demand can be thought of as being the arithmetic mean level of demand. We could express this concept of average in terms of some other measure of "average". We could, for example, suggest that the band 225–250 should be regarded as being a reasonable average because it represents the most likely (or frequent) level of demand. In statistics, this most likely level is described as the *modal level*. In our study of probability we shall prefer the *expected value* measure of *average* because it is a concept which is widely used in the decision-theory analysis discussed in later chapters.

Before we move on from the idea of a probability distribution we should indicate that there are quantitative measures available which describe the degree of spread or variability in a distribution. The measure of spread which is most widely used is the *standard deviation*. The standard deviation is the measure which describes the spread of the observations about the arithmetic mean or expected value of the distribution. When interpreting the variability of the distribution of some uncertain quantity it is valuable to express the standard deviation as a percentage of the expected value. A distribution with a high value for this percentage is much more variable than one with a low-percentage value.

We do not take up here the procedures involved in calculating standard deviations. Reference should be made to an elementary statistics text such as Moroney[1]. All that the reader needs in order to follow the methods in this book is an understanding of what the standard deviation measures, i.e. variability and an appreciation of how to interpret it in relation to particular distributions for uncertain quantities of interest.

The final topic which we must take up in our broad canvas of probability concepts is the theorem which is extremely useful in certain decision-theory applications. This theorem, called Bayes' theorem, has given the intellectual impetus for a number of theoretical statisticians and decision analysts who work in the decision-theory area to develop the Bayesian school of decision theory. The main Bayesian analysts, such as Raiffa, Schlaifer and Pratt, form an extremely powerful group who work on decision-theory problems and applications at the Harvard Business School.

Bayes' Theorem

The essential logic of Bayes' theorem is quite simple. In formal terms it is an extension of the basic notion of conditional probability but in practical terms it is of tremendous value in decision-theory applications. Consider the situation in which a decision-maker in a car firm makes a set of assessments about the demand level for a new product (see Table 1.6 again for an example of such a situation). Suppose that, despite his conviction about his initial *prior* assessments of the probabilities of occurrence of various demand levels, he decides to commission a market-research survey to find out the likely reaction of a panel of consumers to the new product. His aim is to get some concrete evidence to help him revise and refine his initial *prior* assessments about demand levels. Bayes' theorem is a mechanism which combines sample evidence of the market-research type with the *prior* assessments in order to obtain a series of *posterior* assessments which are *revised* probability assessments of demand for a new product. We will illustrate this theorem by means of an example which illustrates as simply as possible the principles involved. First of all, however, we shall formally state Bayes' theorem. To do this we identify the following steps:

1 Let some experiment lead to a set of n possible mutually exclusive outcomes, i.e. $A_1, A_2, \ldots A_i, \ldots A_n$ (e.g. A_1 might be *high sales*, A_2 *medium sales* and A_3 *low sales*—in this case there would only be *three* outcomes).

2 The *prior probability* of $A_i = P(A_i)$ is obtained for some general event A_i (note: i can take on values from 1 to n in the experiment).

This prior probability is an expression, in terms of one of the probability concepts previously discussed, of the decision-maker's prior assessment of the probability of the occurrence of event A_i.

3 We perform some random experiment or obtain some evidence about the occurrence of event B conditional on the prior states $A_1, \ldots A_n$, i.e. we obtain probabilities $P(B/A_i)$.

4 We revise the probability of A_i based on the condition that we have observed the occurrence of the event B.

This revised probability, called the *posterior probability*, $P(A_i/B)$ is given by *Bayes' theorem*, i.e.

$$P(A_i/B) = \frac{P(A_i)B(B/A_i)}{P(A_1)P(B/A_1) + P(A_2)P(B/A_2) + \ldots + P(A_n)P(B/A_n)}$$

In words Bayes' theorem says that the posterior probability of some event A_i after observing some evidence B is proportional to the product of the prior probability of A_i and the conditional probability (or likelihood) of B given A_i.

This complicated-looking formula must seem pretty indigestible. The best cure for indigestion in this situation is an example:

EXAMPLE

A certain company is in the process of launching a new car. The marketing director assigns a subjective probability of 0·9 to the event "the car is superior to its immediate competitor". However, he is not sure if his assessment is correct because of his total commitment to, and enthusiasm for, the new car. He calls up a reputable market-research company and asks for a quick survey to confirm or reject his initial prior assessment. The market-research executive reminds his client that his survey will only be 80 per cent reliable because of the potential extent of measurement and sampling errors. In operational terms 80 per cent reliability means the following: the survey will indicate either *superiority* or *inferiority* of the new car; if the car is really superior the survey will indicate superiority with probability of 0·8 and, similarly, if the car is really inferior the survey will indicate inferiority with probability 0·8.

The marketing director wants the market-research firm to tell him what his revised probability assessment for the event "the car is superior to its immediate competitor" should be after the completion of the survey.

Bayes' theorem seems to be the logical mechanism for obtaining revised probabilities in this situation. Let us therefore try to apply it.

First of all, we shall write down the information given to us in the example:

Let the event E_1 denote "new car is *superior* to its immediate competitor" and also let the event E_2 denote "new car is *inferior* to its immediate competitor".

1 Prior probabilities are given as follows, i.e. the decision-maker's prior assessments are

$$P(E_1) = 0.9 \quad P(E_2) = 0.1$$

2 Let Z_1 denote the event "market-research survey indicates that the new car is superior to its immediate competitor"
and Z_2 denote the event "market research survey indicates that the new car is inferior to its immediate competitor".
The conditional probabilities can then be expressed as follows:

$$P(Z_1/E_1) = 0.8 \quad P(Z_1/E_2) = 0.2$$
$$P(Z_2/E_1) = 0.2 \quad P(Z_2/E_2) = 0.8$$

3 The revised or posterior probability that the new car is superior to its competitor (conditional on the indication from the survey that it is superior) is given by Bayes' theorem

$$P(E_1/Z_1) = \frac{0.9 \times 0.8}{0.9 \times 0.8 + 0.1 \times 0.2}$$

$$= \frac{0.72}{0.74} \simeq \underline{\underline{0.97}}$$

From this final figure 0.97 we can say that, if the market-research findings indicate that the new car is superior, the marketing director's posterior assessment for the probability of the new car being superior should be 0.97, i.e. very close to "certainty".

It can be seen from this example that Bayes' theorem is extremely useful for obtaining revised probability assessments in those decision situations in which the decision-maker has the option of collecting some additional evidence. However, there are many decision situations, particularly in investment decision-making, in which it is difficult to collect relevant additional evidence. In these situations we have to rely considerably upon the accuracy of the decision-maker's initial or prior probability assessments. It is necessary, therefore, to discuss methods by which we can obtain reliable and accurate prior probability assessments from decision-makers.

Assessment of Subjective Probability Distributions from Decision-makers

Let us consider an investment decision-making situation as a means of illustrating the range of methods available for the assessment of subjective probability distributions. Suppose that the executives of a food company ABC must decide about launching a new instant potato product. They have concluded that the rate of return they can expect from the product is a function of five uncertain quantities (UQ's): advertising expenditures, total market for instant potato, ABC's share of the total market, investment costs and length of life of instant potato as a consumer product. After getting single most likely estimates of each of these quantities, the accountant calculates the discounted rate of return and finds a healthy return of 25 per cent. If, however, the decision-makers assign, say, a 50 per cent probability of obtaining the correct values for each of the five uncertain quantities, there is only a (0·5 × 0·5 × 0·5 × 0·5 × 0·5) 3 per cent chance that all five estimates will be correct. This means that the attainment of a 25 per cent rate of return is dependent on a rather unlikely state of affairs, i.e. 3 per cent chance of all the estimates being correct. This simple example illustrates that the decision-maker needs to know the approximate probability distribution of values for each uncertain quantity and how combinations of values from each probability distribution will interact to form a probability distribution for the rate of return criterion.

Suppose now that we accept that we should try to find probability distributions rather than point estimates for the values of uncertain quantities. The problem is then how to obtain meaningful probabilistic estimates for uncertain quantities from practical decision-makers.

Perhaps the simplest approach is to ask the decision-maker to specify the high, low and most likely values for the uncertain quantities. Such three-level estimates are useful in helping to provide a rough picture of the appropriate probability distribution but they do not go far enough in approximating the entire shape of the probability distribution.

In Table 1.9 we show how some decision-makers approximate the probability distribution in terms of the low, most likely and high values for the uncertain quantity (UQ) of interest. Suppose that investment cost is the appropriate (UQ) and that the decision-maker is asked to specify ranges within which each value (low, most likely, high) is likely to occur and the odds (or probability assessments) he will assign to each of these ranges.

TABLE 1.9

Approximation of Probability Distribution from Decision-maker's Assessments

(a) Table of Assessments by Decision-maker

Investment cost (£ million)	Probability (or odds)	Probability per £0·1 (to two figures)
Low Range 0·65–0·8	0·2	0·13
Most Likely Range 0·8–1·1	0·65	0·22
High Range 1·1–2·0	0·15	0·02

(b) Associated Probability Distribution

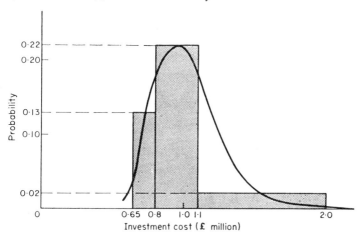

Note: the area under the curve of this probability distribution is 1 by virtue of the method of constructing the histogram.

In this case we can see that the distribution has a shape which is *skewed* to the right, i.e. the distribution is not symmetrical about the vertical axis. In practical terms this indicates that investment costs of 0·65 to 1·1 million pounds are much more likely to happen than extremely high values between 1·1 and 2 million pounds.

Alternative assumptions about the form of the probability distribution can, of course, be made. An equally popular assumption is to assume that the *low, most likely* and *high* values can be used to form a triangular distribution.

Although such assumptions about the form of probability distributions are commonly made by practical decision analysts and can be useful in certain circumstances, we do not feel that we should encourage their widespread use. In assessing a probability distribution the approach should always be to measure the *entire* shape of the distribution as accurately as possible. In operational terms this means that decision-makers should be asked to draw the probability distributions for each uncertain quantity under the guidance of a decision analyst.

A procedure for obtaining a probability distribution for an uncertain quantity (UQ) must start by ensuring that the decision-maker understands the relevant concepts of probability theory and, in particular, is aware of the meaning attached to a probability distribution. Once the decision-maker appreciates what is meant by a probability assessment he must be given access to all the information about the uncertain quantity which the firm has available, e.g. accounting records, sales figures and market-research information. He should then form his degrees of belief about the uncertain quantity on the basis of the mix of information and subjective feelings. In the process of setting down the form of the probability distribution for each UQ the presence of a decision analyst is often very useful. The approach of the decision analyst in this dialogue is to ask the decision-maker questions such as:

"At what value of the UQ, $\bar{U}$, do you feel that there is a 50/50 chance that the true value of the UQ will be below $\bar{U}$?"

This question establishes the value of the UQ, $\bar{U}$, up to which the area under the curve is one-half of the total area, i.e. $\frac{1}{2}$.

By a process of changing the questions the decision analyst can derive several points on the probability distribution. Once these points have been obtained, a smoothed curve can be drawn through them to give a pretty accurate description of the decision-maker's probability distribution on the UQ.

The previous discussion should have convinced the reader that the process of obtaining a probability assessment is a complex and difficult one. There is no adequate short cut if accurate and reliable probability assessments are to be obtained from decision-makers. Each decision-maker must have adequate training in probability concepts and exposure to all relevant information about the UQ of interest.

Any reader who wants to take the subject further should refer to the excellent discussion in Raiffa[2].

Probability, Uncertainty and Decision Problems

The notions of probability concepts and uncertainty have been introduced because they are one of the basic building blocks for the analysis of decision. To illustrate the directions in which the subsequent chapters are leading, this chapter ends by providing two capsule descriptions of important business-decision problems undertaken in an environment of uncertainty, i.e. the new product decision and the research and development programme decision problem.

(A) THE NEW PRODUCT DECISION PROBLEM

The marketing manager is often faced with decisions about whether to proceed with the launch of a new product once the development work on it has been satisfactorily completed. Some of the major variables that will affect his decision are the likely extent of market penetration of the product, the likely extent of competition in the market and the amount of promotional expenditures necessary to ensure an effective product launch. Further, the decision-maker is uncertain about the time for which he can expect an adequate sales volume for the product and the associated problem of how long a competitive advantage may be maintained in the face of potential competition.

The decision-maker can reduce some of these dimensions of uncertainty by instituting information-gathering programmes. For example, he can commission a market survey from a market-research organization and assess the likely levels of demand at prices within a feasible price range.

Nevertheless, he cannot reduce uncertainty completely and must make a decision in the context of this uncertain environment. How should the decision-maker resolve his problem?

(B) THE RESEARCH AND DEVELOPMENT DECISION: EVALUATION OF A POTENTIAL PROJECT

In certain sectors of industry one of the major determinants of a firm's profitability and growth is the effectiveness of its research and development activity. Any firm which is actively engaged in R & D is faced with periodic decisions about the viability of potential research projects generated within the firm. In such a decision situation the decision-maker is faced with two alternative strategies. First, he can decide to accept or reject a project on the basis of information at present available. Second, he can postpone an immediate decision and proceed with the development work on every project until more information about its ultimate success becomes available, e.g. unforeseen technical difficulties, etc. Each of these strategies may be complicated because decisions on the acceptance of new projects may have to be made in competition with decisions about the continuation of existing projects within the research and development programme. In any event the evaluation of any project must consider its likely development cost, its possible future market penetration at a given price and the extent of possible competition in the research area under consideration. In addition, the time period necessary for the development work must be considered fully if the firm is unwilling to commit financial resources to projects which do not produce payoff over a sufficiently short period of time.

Under the second strategy, i.e. the postponement strategy, the firm can reduce uncertainty at a given cost, the cost of development until the next review period, by postponing the immediate "go/no go" decision.

The decision-maker is thus in an uncertain decision situation which is often made more difficult because of the dynamically changing character of technical knowledge. How should he proceed?

SUMMARY AND REVIEW

The purpose of this chapter has been to introduce the basic ideas and concepts of probability. Probability concepts, particularly the idea of subjective probability as a state of mind, are widely used in operational research and decision analysis models. Indeed, as this book proceeds, it will become evident that a great deal of the promise of decision theory lies in the decision-maker's ability to make subjective assessments of the uncertain factors in his decision problem. These might, for example, in a particular case be the demand levels after the launch of a new product and the price at which the new product should be sold.

An equally important concept is the probability density function or distribution. For example, if a decision-maker assesses subjective probabilities for sales levels (say high, medium or low) he will generally not give a probability assessment of 1·0, i.e. "certainty", to any one of the levels. This is because he feels that there is some chance that any one of the levels may occur, even though he may be pretty sure, say, that sales will be at the medium level. The set of sales levels, high, medium and low, together with their associated probabilities of occurrence, define a probability distribution for sales. It might be:

	Probability
high sales (£1 mill.) volume	0·2
medium sales (£0·5 mill.) volume	0·6
low sales (£0·25 mill.) volume	0·2

When the decision-maker assesses a probability distribution such as the one above, he naturally askes himself two questions:

"What is the average or expected sales level?"
"How variable is the distribution?"

In this case the average sales level is $0.2 \times 1 + 0.6 \times 0.5 + 0.2 \times 0.25 = £0.55$ mill.

Though we did not discuss how to calculate the spread of the distribution, we indicated that the important thing was to be able to interpret the value of the measure of spread in relation to the average sales level. The measure of spread, used in this case, namely the standard deviation, has a value of 0.07 million. The variability as a proportion of the average sales level $\frac{0.07}{0.54} = 13$ per cent indicates that the distribution is fairly concentrated about the average level.

The other important notion in the chapter is Bayes' theorem. Bayes' theorem is a mechanism for revising prior probability assessments with the aid of new evidence into a set of posterior probability assessments. An example in the chapter shows how posterior assessments of demand levels are evaluated by using the results obtained from a market-research survey.

The main problem in using the ideas of probability in decision problems is getting meaningful assessments of probabilities for uncertain quantities such as sales from decision-makers. Decision-makers often find it difficult to express their feelings about uncertainties in probabilistic terms and this means that great efforts must be made to train and acquaint decision-makers with the basic simplicity and logic of probabilistic thinking.

Review the Following Concepts

For the decision analysis material which follows in subsequent chapters the reader will find it necessary to have an appreciation of the following concepts:

(i) *The meaning of probability and particularly subjective probability.* The reader should be aware of the properties of a probability measure and the rules for getting probabilities of both simple and compound events.

(ii) *The probability-tree diagram.* This versatile concept for getting the probabilities of compound events is basically similar in concept and logic to the decision-tree diagram we introduce in subsequent chapters.

(iii) The idea of a *probability distribution* and measures of mean and spread such as the *expected value* and *standard deviation* should be studied. The expected-value concept is important because of its wide use in decision analysis.

(iv) *Bayes' theorem* should be seen as a mechanism for revising prior probability assessments.

(v) Methods for obtaining *assessments of probabilities* from decision-makers are also of major importance.

References

1. Moroney, M. J., *Facts From Figures*, Penguin Books, Harmondsworth, 1955.
2. Raiffa, H., *Decision Analysis*, Addison-Wesley, Reading, Mass., 1968.

2   *The Structure of Decision Problems*

Decision-making as a process is an amalgam of both rational and psychological factors. Decision-theory analysis studies the *rational* factor in order to clarify the way in which decisions should be made. However, the analysis does not make the decision-maker's role superfluous. The decision-maker, having analysed the decision problem normatively via decision-theory analysis, must introspectively apply the blend of rational and psychological factors in order to come to a decision about the problem under consideration.

In our study, therefore, we shall outline the procedures for rational decision-making known collectively as decision-theory analysis. We shall show the underlying logic of *decision-tree diagrams* and develop the logic to obtain an analytical method for determining the best strategy to adopt in a given decision problem.

It should be noted initially that the method of decision-theory analysis is more than just one of the techniques that we could use to throw light upon a given decision problem. What we hope to show in this book is that decision-theory analysis provides a framework for the logical analysis of any business-decision problem. We will show by example how decision-theory analysis makes the decision-maker aware of the elements in his decision problem and the various possible strategies that he must consider.

Structure of a Decision Problem

In essence, therefore, we are saying that decision problems have a structure and that decision analysis forces the decision-maker to recognize the structure. The structure of a representative decision problem has some or all of the following elements.

First, the decision-maker has a set of objectives whose realization depends upon the decision he takes. Examples of objectives are profits, market share, increase in turnover, etc. Essentially, an objective is a target which a decision-maker is hoping to achieve. In some cases there will be only a single objective though in most real-life situations there are many objectives and there may be conflicts in achieving satisfactory amounts of each of them. For example, an increase in profits might be achieved at the expense of a reduction in market share, particularly if pricing policy is used as a means of obtaining a short-term profit gain. Clearly, decision theory should provide a method for analysing such interdependencies between objectives in order that the opportunity cost of taking any particular decision may be seen.

Second, the decision-maker has a set of alternative courses of action (or strategies) which he can adopt in a particular decision-problem context. For example, the decision problem may be concerned with the location and size of a new plant. His courses of action could be, first, to carry on with the existing plant or, second, to invest in new plant at one of a set of locations (e.g. Scotland, Wales and Northern Ireland) with one of a set of possible levels of investment (£1 million, £2 million, £3 million, etc.).

Third, decision problems always exist in an uncertain environment. The decision to launch a new product has to be made even though variables such as the behaviour of competitors, or consumers' reaction to the new product which affect the firm's situation, are not known with certainty. In effect the decision to launch the product can be likened to a game against "nature" where "nature" is understood loosely as being a mechanism which generates events in the real world. For example, if we launch the product we may face the immediate possibility of a similar product being launched at a lower price. Such a possibility is one of the set of states of nature which may result if we decide to launch the new product. The important point is that the combination of the selection of the specific strategy of launching the new product by the decision-maker, and the occurrence of a specific state of nature such as a competitor introducing a similar product at a lower price, will result in a particular outcome, let us say a loss on the new product.

Fourth, therefore, the quantity that we need in an analysis of a decision problem is a measure of the *value* of this loss or outcome in terms of the decision-maker's objectives. Let us call this measure of value *utility*. In many situations the natural measure for utility is *money profit* though it does not necessarily reflect exactly the true measure of the outcome (in utility terms) in terms of the decision-maker's objectives. To illustrate this point suppose that you, the reader, were offered the following gamble: A coin is tossed, and if

32

it comes up heads you win £100 but if it comes up tails you lose £50. Should you accept the gamble?

A statistician would probably answer the question as follows: The probability of getting either a head or a tail on a toss of a coin is equal because, assuming that the coin is unbiased, i.e. has not been the subject of artificial loading, the occurrence of either outcome is equally likely. Therefore, if your decision criterion is to maximize expected profit, the logical thing to do is to accept the gamble. The calculation is given below:

(a) probability of head = probability of tail = $\frac{1}{2}$
(b) expected profit = $\frac{1}{2} \times £100 + \frac{1}{2} \times -£50$
                = £25

The expected profit criterion really says that you will expect to get £100 half of the time and lose £50 half of the time. The net gain in the long run is thus £25. However, it is fair to ask whether you would always accept the offer. The answer to this question is very much dependent upon your financial position. If the £50 loss has minimal effect on your finances you will probably prefer to gamble. Now if you have only £100 in the bank and you need it for some urgent bills then you would probably prefer to avoid the gamble as far as possible. In the latter situation the risk of losing means more to you than the chance of winning whereas the situation is reversed in the former case. Only when the decision-maker is indifferent to either loss or gain can it be said that expected monetary value (or profit), *EMV*, is the correct decision criterion.

So far we have identified *objectives, strategies, states of nature* and *payoffs* (or value measures) as common elements of the structure of any decision problem. We can identify these elements in the situation just described in which the decision-maker is offered the choice of a gamble between two monetary amounts conditional upon the toss of a coin. The strategies are "gamble/don't gamble", the states of nature are "win/lose", the *payoffs* are £100 and −£50 and the objective of the decision-maker is to maximize utility. In many cases utility is measured by profit, though, as we have seen in the gambling situation, the decision-maker's objective is conditioned by the level of resources that he has available. If the decision-maker is indifferent to either gain or loss, then expected profit is the optimal decision criterion.

The structure of this decision problem can be represented in terms of a payoff matrix shown in Table 2.1.

It becomes clear on looking at the table that the analysis of the decision, i.e. whether or not to gamble, must depend upon the

TABLE 2.1

Payoff Matrix for Gambling Problem

| | States of nature | |
	$(\frac{1}{2})$ Win	$(\frac{1}{2})$ Lose
Strategies		
Gamble	£100	−£50
Don't gamble	£0	£0

Note: the entries in the matrix represent the payoffs from each strategy/state of nature combination.

decision-maker's knowledge about the likelihood of occurrence of the states of nature. In this case the probability distribution on the states of nature *win* or *lose* is known, i.e. the probability of winning or losing is $\frac{1}{2}$. When the probability distribution on the states of nature is known we have a *risky* situation. Most business situations, however, are uncertain situations because the decision-maker has no objective knowledge of the probabilities on the states of nature. Consider once again a new product launch. Before the launch, assuming that the product is unique, the marketing manager probably has very little hard information about "nature" other than subjective feelings or the results of *ad hoc* surveys from market research companies. Business-decision situations are, therefore, analysed in an environment which is *uncertain*. If, by chance, the decision-maker knows with certainty which action "nature" will take, then the decision problem is solved immediately. All the decision-maker has to do is to choose the strategy for the given state of nature which will maximize his gain.

It is always the case that business-decision problems are either risk or uncertainty problems. In these risk and uncertainty situations we need to consider what criterion the decision-maker should adopt in selecting the optimal strategy. At the present time decision theory provides no one best criterion for selecting a strategy under conditions of uncertainty. This is because what is best is often determined by the decision-maker's attitudes and the norms or policies laid down by the firm which employs him. However, a number of alternative criteria which express different decision-making attitudes have been developed and we will explain the rationale underlying each one. It should be clear that different attitudes may lead to the selection of different strategies. We should accept any decision as long as a rational criterion which expresses a particular attitudinal framework is used in its determination.

Decision Criteria

We shall illustrate these alternative criteria in terms of a decision problem under uncertainty. In such a problem the decision-maker's choice of a strategy does not influence the state of nature which occurs. Take, for example, the following decision problem. Mr Z has £x to invest and his bank manager suggests that he has three options available to him. First, to invest in ordinary shares. Second, to invest in unit trusts. Third, to invest in a building society deposit account. The yield (%) which he will gain under each option will depend upon the present and future state of the economy. Mr Z is further advised that *growth*, *stagnation* and *decline* are the states of the British economy which he should consider in his analysis. After further discussion with his financial advisers, Mr Z assigns estimated yields to each strategy and state of nature combination. The structure of the decision problem is represented below in the now familiar decision matrix table:

TABLE 2.2

Mr Z's Decision Problem

	State of economy		
	Growth	Stagnation	Decline
a_1 ordinary shares	20	1	−6
a_2 unit trusts	10	6	0
a_3 building society	4	4	4

MAXIMIN OR PESSIMISM

Faced with the decision problem, Mr Z might take a pessimistic view of the prospects for the economy. A rational course of action under these circumstances would be to assume that nature will always act to give him the minimum payoff and he should, therefore, select his strategy to get as large a payoff as possible under these circumstances. We call this strategy the MAXIMIN strategy because it *maxi*mizes the *mini*mum payoff.

TABLE 2.3

Illustration of Maximin for Mr Z's Decision Problem

	Minimum payoff
a_1	−6
a_2	0
a_3	4 $\longrightarrow$ ACTION a_3—invest in building society deposits— maximizes the minimum payoff

Thus, under this completely pessimistic maximin criterion first suggested by Wald[1] he should choose the building society investment option. This is because the building society option is best when "nature" is worst, i.e. when the economy is declining (see Table 2.3).

MAXIMAX OR OPTIMISM

On the other hand, the decision-maker may be a complete optimist and assume that nature will always be favourable, i.e. will always act to give him the maximum payoff. He should then choose the strategy which *maxi*mizes the *maxi*mum payoff (obtained under the growth phase). The calculation in Table 2.4 shows that the maximax strategy should be to invest in ordinary shares.

TABLE 2.4

Illustration of Maximax for Mr Z's Decision Problem

	Maximum payoff	
a_1	20 ⟶	ACTION a_1—invest in ordinary shares—maxi-
a_2	10	mizes the maximum payoff
a_3	4	

MIXTURES OF OPTIMISM AND PESSIMISM (Hurwicz)

Because pure attitudes of optimism and pessimism are extreme, decision theorists such as Hurwicz[2] have suggested mixed "optimistic-pessimistic" strategies. However, mixed strategies, though intuitively appealing, are difficult to apply because of the problems involved in determining the relative weights to be given to the pessimistic and optimistic cases. The decision-maker, in these cases, has to assign weights of coefficients of optimism and pessimism which reflect his feelings about the relative likelihoods of occurrence of the maximum and minimum payoffs. Suppose that the decision-maker, Mr Z, assigns equal weights to the occurrence of each of the maximum and minimum payoffs. Then a mixed Hurwicz-type decision criterion would suggest that investment in ordinary shares is the best strategy (see Table 2.5).

Regret (or Opportunity Loss) Criterion

Savage[3] argues that it is more natural for decision-makers to think in terms of opportunity costs (or losses) rather than yields (or profits). Suppose that Mr Z chose to invest in ordinary shares without the help of any formal decision criteria. If the economy goes through a growth phase he will have made the correct choice and in retrospect will feel no opportunity loss or regret. However, if either stagnation or decline occurs then Mr Z's choice would have been incorrect. In both of these cases, therefore, the decision-maker experienced an opportunity loss (or regret) measured by the difference between the yield under Mr Z's choice and the yield under the optimal choice for the given state of nature. In other words, an opportunity loss is the loss incurred because of failure to take the best action available.

TABLE 2.5

Illustration of Hurwicz Criterion for Mr Z's Decision Problem

Probabilities of:	(0·5)	(0·5)	
	Maximum payoff	Minimum payoff	Hurwicz values
a_1	20	−6	7——▶a_1
a_2	10	0	5
a_3	4	4	4

Note: (1) The weights (i.e. coefficients of optimism and pessimism) sum to 1
(2) the Hurwicz values in Column 3 are obtained as follows:

for a_1: Hurwicz = Maximum payoff × weight of maximum payoff
+ Minimum payoff × weight of minimum payoff,
i.e.
= $(20 \times 0·5) + (-6 \times 0·5) = 10 - 3 = \underline{\underline{7}}$

Similarly
for a_2: Hurwicz = $(10 \times 0·5) + (0 \times 0·5) = 5 + 0 = \underline{\underline{5}}$

a_3: Hurwicz = $(4 \times 0·5) + (4 \times 0·5) = 2 + 2 = \underline{\underline{4}}$

To firm our understanding of the opportunity-loss concept we shall transform our original payoff matrix (see Table 2.2) into an opportunity loss matrix. For a given state of nature, e.g. growth, the opportunity loss of an act is the difference between the payoff of that act and payoff for the best act that could have been selected. Thus, for growth, a_1 (invest in ordinary shares) is the best act. For a_1 the regret or opportunity loss is $20 - 20 = 0$, i.e. for a_1 the act selected and the best act coincide given that growth is the state of nature. For a_2, in the same situation of growth, the opportunity loss is $20 - 10 = 10$ units and for a_3 the opportunity loss is $20 - 4 = 16$ units. It should be noted that it is a matter of convention for opportunity losses to be presented as positive.

In a similar manner the opportunity losses, given stagnation and decline situations, can be calculated. The opportunity loss (or regret) matrix for Mr Z's decision problem is shown in Table 2.6.

TABLE 2.6

Mr Z's Regret (or Opportunity Loss) Matrix

	Growth	Stagnation	Decline
a_1	0	5	10
a_2	10	0	4
a_3	16	2	0

Note: the payoff matrix for Mr Z is presented in Table 2.2.

With this regret matrix we can now apply pessimistic or optimistic rules to the regret matrix. For example, we could argue that it is always in the individual's best interests to be completely pessimistic about nature. In this situation we should minimax regret, i.e. we should make the opportunity losses as small as possible. The best strategy under these circumstances is to buy ordinary shares (see Table 2.7).

TABLE 2.7

Illustration of Minimax Regret Criterion for Mr Z's Decision Problem

Strategy	Worst or MAXIMUM regret (opportunity loss)
a_1	0 ← a_1—investment in ordinary shares—minimizes the
a_2	10 maximum possible opportunity loss
a_3	16

The decision criteria which have been considered so far have not looked explicitly at the relative probabilities of the occurrence of the possible states of nature. Nevertheless, a pessimistic attitude on the part of a decision-maker would suggest a particular probability weighting for the states of nature and a particular attitude of the decision-maker towards the avoidance of loss.

In general, the choice of a criterion (or a *decision rule*) for the selection of the optimal strategy in a decision problem is a function of the uncertainty inherent in the decision problem and the attitude of the decision-maker towards that uncertainty. Uncertainty itself implies that the decision-maker is sensitive to the two elements of payoff: financial return and the uncertainty attached to financial return (which can be expressed in terms of uncertainties about the states of nature which are important in the particular decision problem). Attitude towards uncertainty is reflected in many cases in the transformation of the money payoff values to utility values which measure the subjective satisfaction derived by the decision-maker from each of the possible consequences of the decision problem. We saw earlier in the gambling example that long-run profit is not necessarily a good decision rule because it implies that the decision-maker is indifferent to either outcome of the gamble—gain or loss.

Bayes' Decision Strategy

A series of alternative decision criteria, known as Bayes' strategies, have been developed using the concept of a subjective probability distribution on the states of nature. This probability distribution reflects the individual decision-maker's assessments of the likelihood of occurrence of the various possible states of nature. The Bayes strategy is to maximize expected monetary value, EMV, i.e. to choose that strategy which maximizes the payoff weighted by the probability distribution on the states of nature, or minimizes expected opportunity loss, EOL, where this means the opportunity loss weighted by the probability distribution on the states of nature. It can be shown that this strategy applied to the payoff (yield) matrix or the loss matrix will lead to the same decision, i.e. it will pick the same strategy from the subset of possible strategies.

We illustrate the Bayes strategies in Tables 2.8 and 2.9 applied to both the payoff matrix (see Table 2.2) and the loss matrix (see Table 2.6) for Mr Z's decision problems. In both cases the states of nature, i.e. growth, stagnation and decline, are assumed to have an equal chance of occurring. This means that the probability of stagnation = probability of growth = probability of decline = $\frac{1}{3}$. This assumption is a realistic one for a decision-maker if he has no grounds or feelings for believing that any one of the states of nature is more likely to happen.

TABLE 2.8

Illustration of the EMV Strategy for Mr Z's Decision Problem

$$
\begin{aligned}
EMV\,(a_1) &= (\tfrac{1}{3} \times 20) + (\tfrac{1}{3} \times 1) + (\tfrac{1}{3} \times -6) = 5 \\
EMV\,(a_2) &= (\tfrac{1}{3} \times 10) + (\tfrac{1}{3} \times 6) + (\tfrac{1}{3} \times 0) \;\;= 5\tfrac{1}{3} \longleftarrow \\
EMV\,(a_3) &= (\tfrac{1}{3} \times 4) + (\tfrac{1}{3} \times 4) + (\tfrac{1}{3} \times 4) \;\;= 4
\end{aligned}
$$

Note: Strategy a_2 is selected because it maximizes EMV.

TABLE 2.9

Illustration of the EOL Strategy for Mr Z's Decision Problem

$$
\begin{aligned}
EOL\,(a_1) &= (\tfrac{1}{3} \times 0) + (\tfrac{1}{3} \times 5) + (\tfrac{1}{3} \times 10) = 5 \\
EOL\,(a_2) &= (\tfrac{1}{3} \times 10) + (\tfrac{1}{3} \times 0) + (\tfrac{1}{3} \times 4) = 4\tfrac{2}{3} \longleftarrow \\
EOL\,(a_3) &= (\tfrac{1}{3} \times 16) + (\tfrac{1}{3} \times 2) + (\tfrac{1}{3} \times 0) = 6
\end{aligned}
$$

Note: Strategy a_2 is selected because it minimizes EOL.

This demonstration, using the payoff and loss tables for the investment example, has shown that the Bayes strategies of minimizing *EOL* and maximizing *EMV* are equivalent in the sense of selecting the same strategy. If subjective probabilities can be obtained to represent the uncertainties about the states of nature then it can always be shown that the Bayes strategy is the rational strategy to select in a given decision problem.

Which Decision Criterion Is Best?

The reader is now probably thoroughly confused after the introduction of a wide-ranging set of alternative decision criteria as to which decision criterion is the most operationally useful one. You are probably asking why the problem of which decision criterion to use cannot be formulated as a decision problem and solved using decision theory. Decision theory is a useful formal mechanism but it cannot allow completely for the dimensions of the decision-maker's attitudes and objectives. We suggest, and explain in subsequent chapters, that the Bayes strategies offer the most sensible approximations for decision-makers, particularly if decision-makers are willing to assign subjective probabilities to the states of nature considered appropriate in a given decision problem. We therefore base our discussion in subsequent chapters on the Bayesian *EMV* or expected payoff criterion; and we shall regard this to be the rational decision rule in a decision problem. We shall see once more that it may be sensible to replace payoff by utility in situations where the decision-maker is not indifferent to gain or loss.

SUMMARY

In this chapter we have introduced our study of decision-theory analysis. Decision theory should be regarded as a formal structure for the analysis of decision problems. In this formal structure we can identify *objectives*, *strategies*, *states of nature* and *payoffs* (or value measures) as being the elements which characterize a decision problem. In any decision problem, however, we require to find a *decision rule* or criterion by means of which we can select the optimal strategy to undertake. Our discussion showed that many possible criteria have been suggested for the analysis of decision problems but we strongly recommend that the Bayes strategy of maximization of expected monetary value (or minimizing *EOL*) is the most realistic operational strategy, particularly if we force the decision-maker to make subjective probability assessments for the uncertain states of nature.

In the next chapter we will put further flesh upon the skeleton structure of a decision problem that we have developed. In particular, we must consider the decision-tree concept as an alternative means for representing the structure of a decision problem.

Review of Essential Concepts

(i) Review the *payoff matrix* representation of a decision problem. In Mr Z's simplified decision problem he had three possible options open to him:

a_1: investment in ordinary shares;
a_2: investment in unit trusts;
a_3: investment in building society shares,

and was uncertain about the state of the economy, i.e. growth, stagnation or decline. He estimated certain yields or payoffs for each strategy conditional upon the states of the economy. His payoff matrix was then given as follows:

States of Nature

		Growth	Stagnation	Decline
	a_1	20	1	−6
Acts or	a_2	10	6	0
Strategies	a_3	4	4	4

The general structure of a payoff matrix is thus:

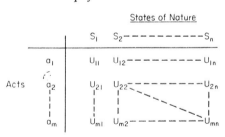

where $a_1, a_2 \ldots a_m$ are the m possible acts, where m is any positive number
$S_1, S_2 \ldots S_n$ are the n possible states of nature, where n is any positive number

and $U_{m1}, \ldots U_{mn}$ are the payoffs corresponding to specific act/state of nature combinations.

Finally, note in some cases that the decision-maker may also be willing to assign probabilities for the relative odds of occurrence of the states of nature $S_1, \ldots S_n$. We could denote these probabilities as $P_1, \ldots P_n$ where $P_1 + P_2 + \ldots P_n = 1$ from the basic laws of probability.

For example, in Mr Z's decision problem we assigned probability assessments of $\frac{1}{3}$ for each of the possible states (growth, stagnation and decline) under the assumption that we had no information to lead us to suppose that any one of the states was more likely to occur. You, as a reader, may have your own feelings about the probabilities of growth, etc., for the British economy. All this means is that your probability assignments for growth, stagnation and decline may be different from anyone else's but they *must* add up to 1.

(ii) Review also the Bayesian decision rule for the maximization of *EMV* (see Table 2.8) which we shall use in further chapters. Remember at the same time that the alternative decision criteria of pessimism, optimism and mixtures of pessimism and optimism reflect particular attitudes of decision-makers when no objective or subjective information about the states of nature is available.

References

1. Wald, A., *Statistical Decision Functions*, Wiley, 1950.
2. For Hurwicz, L., see White, D. J., *Decision Theory*, Oliver & Boyd, 1969.
3. Savage, L. J., *The Foundations of Statistics*, Wiley, 1954.

3   *The Decision Tree: Concept and Analysis*

I n the previous chapter we discussed decision problems and their structure. We pointed out that most business decisions are made in an uncertain environment and need formal techniques of analysis. Examples of typical business decision problems are:

    (*a*) plant modernization decisions;
    (*b*) decisions about the installation of new manufacturing plant;
    (*c*) decisions about the installation of new computers;
    (*d*) decisions on alternative possible distribution channels;
    (*e*) decisions about introduction of new products;
    (*f*) decisions about allocating the R & D budget to worthy research and development projects.

All of these problems can be regarded as investment-decision problems because in each of them the firm has to make some expenditure which will provide a financial return over some future time horizon, the exact length of which is generally unknown. Uncertainty about the future creates most of the difficulty in such cases and manifests itself in uncertainties about financial rates of return.

In the past, judging from surveys of business use of investment-analysis techniques (see Williams[1], for example), discounted cash flow and present-value methods have not been warmly welcomed or widely used in industry. Most of the criticisms are concerned with the methods themselves which seem to make investment decisions simpler than most businessmen feel they are. To some extent such criticisms are valid if discounted cash flow methods are regarded as being the answer to the businessman's prayers for rationality in decision-making. If, however, they are treated as guidelines for investment decision-making, investment-appraisal formulae can help managers, particularly if they are aware of the limitations inherent in the application of the formulae.

Investment-appraisal formulae are thus one element in the tool-kit of techniques available to decision-makers. In investment-decision problems decision-makers have to distil advice from marketing research, operations research, production and engineering functions as well as financial evaluations of worth supplied by the finance and accounting functions.

Decision-tree analysis provides a structure which a decision-maker can use to integrate the contributions from the various functional areas to the analysis of the decision problem. Instead of over-complicating the analysis the decision-maker is forced to reorganize the alternatives and risks which he faces in investment decision-making and the types of information which can usefully be gathered from experts in the functional areas.

In this chapter we shall discuss the fundamentals of the decision-tree concept and the issues which have to be resolved in order to make it an operational analytic tool. In order to provide an introduction to the more detailed work of this chapter, we shall try to reformulate Mr Z's decision problem (see Chapter 2, Table 2.2) in terms of a decision tree. The payoff table for this problem is presented again below:

TABLE 3.1

Payoff Table for Mr Z's Decision Problem

	Growth	Stagnation	Decline
a_1 ordinary shares	20	1	−6
a_2 unit trusts	10	6	0
a_3 building society	4	4	4

The equivalent decision-tree representation of this decision problem is presented in Table 3.2.

Several points about this decision tree can immediately be made. First, the decision problem illustrated is an example of a *single-stage decision*. There are three alternative decisions, i.e. three strategies a_1, a_2, a_3 which branch out from decision point 1, and three possible states of nature, growth, stagnation and decline which branch out from the chance-event nodes. The selection of the optimal strategy will be obtained by considering all possible decision paths which result from combinations of alternative actions and chance events. Second, once the identification of decision points, alternative actions and uncertain events has been made, i.e. the structure of the tree has been established, the decision-maker has to assign values to

TABLE 3.2

Decision-tree Diagram for Mr Z's Decision Problem

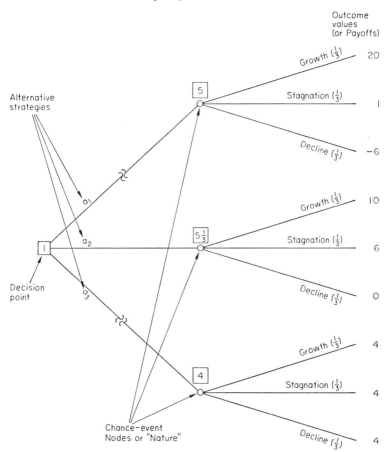

Note: the figures in brackets on the chance event branches represent the values for the probability distribution on the states of nature.

each of the nine end branches of the decision tree. In this case they were assumed as being known to the decision-maker (see the payoff matrix) though in general the determination of the value of specific outcomes can become a complex problem. Third, in many cases probability assignments have to be made for the occurrence of each of the alternative states of nature at a given chance-event node. In this case we have assumed that growth, stagnation and decline are equally likely, and we show the probabilities of their occurrence on the decision tree as being $\frac{1}{3}$ in each case. Fourth, once we have estimated all the values and probabilities needed for the analysis, a criterion for discriminating between the values associated with each course of action has to be developed. In this case we have used the *EMV* criterion (the values of *EMV* for each strategy are given in the square boxes above the chance-events node), and have chosen the unit trust option as being the optimal strategy. Note that we have blocked off the other decision paths by means of the "squiggly" gate ( ) on the basis of their relatively lower *EMV* values.

Therefore, if we accept the *decomposition* of the decision problem into alternative strategies and chance events which affect them as depicted in the tree and agree upon the assignment of probabilities to chance events and values to outcomes, the *EMV* (or some alternative) criterion is the means by which we choose a particular course of action.

We should recognize that this simple single-stage problem brings out most of the concepts inherent in a decision analysis, namely, the decision to be made (decision point 1), the options available (the strategy branches), the uncertain states of nature (the chance-event branches) which affect each option, and the payoffs obtained (end points) from each option/state of nature path. However, most decision problems have a number of stages and a large number of factors that need to be considered. For example, Mr Z in his investment strategy would obviously have the option subsequently of amending his investments in the light of future knowledge about trends in the economy, i.e. he would have a series of subsequent decision points at which he would consider whether to continue with or switch from his present investment policy. In the main body of the chapter we present these multi-stage problems and discuss how we use the method of decision-theory analysis in situations of greater complexity.

The Decision-tree Concept

The decision tree is a means of representing the sequential, multi-stage logic of a decision problem. In any investment-decision situation there are a series of decisions to be made and any action taken now must affect our decisions in the future. Our present decision thus has conditional impact upon future decisions and uncertainties. It sets in motion the flow of activities which characterize the decision problem and provides a logical framework and basis for future decisions. The decision-maker can think of his tree in terms of the elegant analogy suggested by Raiffa[2]. Each path along the decision tree represents a route along which the decision-maker can drive.

Along each route he may have to pay a toll, say the cost of the investment, and will attain different outcomes or rewards through following each route. It is possible that in a complex problem any route will involve a series of costs and benefits and estimation of these quantities may present the decision-maker with a task of great difficulty. Nevertheless, these quantities must be estimated once the decision-maker has *decomposed* the decision problem into its essential elements and imposed the logic of decision-tree analysis on the problem.

The most useful approach for getting the idea of how to draw decision-tree diagrams is to consider the structure of several different investment-decision situations one by one. Let us start by considering a relatively common decision problem. Suppose that the XYZ Company which makes car components is facing heavy demand for one of its products, a revolution counter. As a result of this high-demand situation the managing director and his officers met to consider ways of meeting the demand. Existing plant was working at full capacity on normal shifts and the firm had two options: either to expand capacity by putting all its employees on overtime or to purchase an additional rev. counter assembly machine. It was decided that it was not feasible to subcontract the work out to another supplier because the latter might, as a result, decide to market a competitive instrument with similar technical features itself. Once the two options had been outlined the managing director and his officers discussed what might happen under each alternative course of action. They agreed that the choice between the options was mainly dependent upon what might happen to sales over the one-year planning horizon. They decided that sales would either rise by 15 per cent or fall by 5 per cent, thus excluding any other possibility. They agreed about their probability assessments and decided to assign probabilities of 0·6 (or 60 per cent) to a sales rise of 15 per cent and 0·4 to a sales fall of 5 per cent. They then called in the company accountant and the finance officers to work out the net cash flows, i.e. the net contributions for each option conditional upon the sales level attained. They produced the following payoff table:

TABLE 3.3

Payoff Table (Net Cash Flows) for XYZ Company's Capacity Problem

Probabilities	(0·6) 15% sales rise	(0·4) 5% sales fall
Overtime	+£210,000	+£150,000
Buy new equipment and install	+£220,000	+£130,000

47

Now the payoff table refers only to the payoff over the first year and the decision problem so far represents only a single-stage decision option. However, the marketing manager and the accountant argued strongly against analysing the problem without looking out into the planning horizon beyond the first year. They felt that long-term sales trends for revolution counters were likely to remain in XYZ's favour and that they should extend their analysis to, say, a two-year period. (Note: the choice of a two-year planning horizon is in this case arbitrary and is justified in order to make the exposition of decision-tree concepts as simple as possible. In practical cases, the planning horizon will be an unknown factor and will vary according to the type of decision and the context in which it is taken.) After further discussion the managing director agreed with his colleagues and decided to convene a further meeting to discuss the options open to them over a two-year planning horizon. At that meeting all agreed that they should consider the options open to them and the routes that they could follow in the second year of the planning period. (Note: again this assumption has been made in order to simplify the subsequent analysis. In some cases it is perfectly possible that the decision-maker—or decision-makers—may want to re-structure the tree completely over the whole planning horizon.) After much discussion they decided to set down the problem in terms of a decision tree, the basic structure of which is shown in Table 3.4. Some comments need to be made about this tree. First, that it is obviously oversimplified. It should be clear that there may be several possible actions to evaluate in a given situation and also many uncertainties which have to be considered. However, as we shall see later, it is sensible not to overcomplicate the decision tree if our aim is to understand the essential structure of the decision problem. Second, we have nowhere included in the tree as shown probability assignments for chance events or outcome values for each route along the decision tree. These are refinements which are necessary when we require to arrive at the correct decision and these have to be provided by the decision-makers in the XYZ Company.

Once the marketing manager and the accountant had set down the decision tree as in Table 3.4 and agreed on its structure, they forged ahead with the tasks of making probability assessments for chance event branches and of arriving at valuations for the eighteen end branches of the decision tree.

They decided, first, to consider the difficult task of making probability assessments. Both the marketing director and the accountant felt that the rev. counter had a good long-term sales future. They argued that, even if sales fell over the first year, there would be a probability of 0·8 that sales would at least be medium, i.e. that the

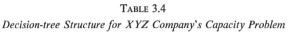

TABLE 3.4

Decision-tree Structure for XYZ Company's Capacity Problem

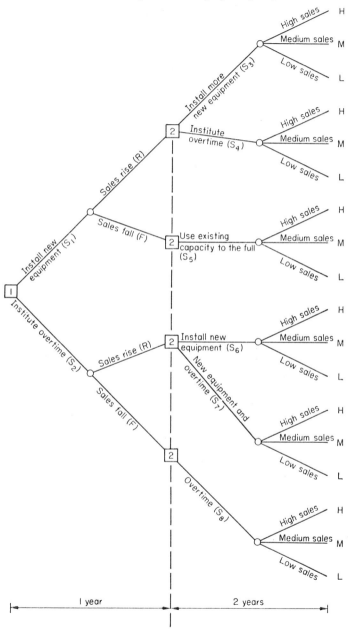

probability of medium sales or high sales would be equal to $\frac{4}{10}$ or 0·4 in each case. Further, if they were lucky enough to get an immediate sales rise in the first year they felt that the trends in the second year would still be in their favour. However, they felt that the probability of medium or high sales would only be 0·3 in each case with a probability of 0·4 of low sales in the second year. Whilst they recognized that the probability assessments were "educated guesses" they nevertheless felt that they gave rough, broad indications of what market trends would be.

The accountant reminded the marketing manager that he would need his help in the estimation of the payoffs (net cash flows) that might accrue if the firm "drove along" each possible chance-event route. The amended decision trees shown in Tables 3.5 and 3.6 present the probability assessments and payoff evaluations that the marketing manager and accountant made.

TABLE 3.5

One-year Decision Tree for XYZ Company's Problem

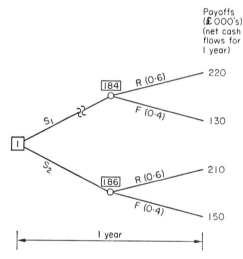

Notes:
    (i) payoffs in this case were given in Table 3.3;
    (ii) strategy S_2—overtime—is selected because of its greater *EMV* value 186 as against 184;
    (iii) *EMV* values for S_1 and S_2 are calculated as follows:
$$EMV(S_1) = 0·6 \times 220 + 0·4 \times 130$$
$$= 132 + 52 = \underline{\underline{184}}$$

$$EMV(S_2) = 0·6 \times 210 + 0·4 \times 150$$
$$= 126 + 60 = \underline{\underline{186}}$$

TABLE 3.6
Two-year Decision Tree for XYZ's Problem

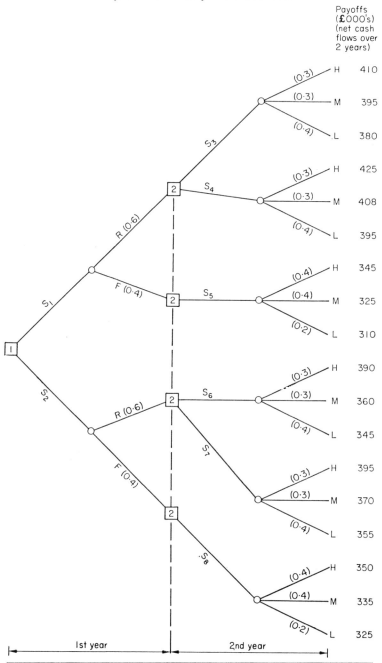

Payoffs
(£000's)
(net cash
flows over
2 years)

H	410
M	395
L	380
H	425
M	408
L	395
H	345
M	325
L	310
H	390
M	360
L	345
H	395
M	370
L	355
H	350
M	335
L	325

1st year   2nd year

Note: The 18 terminal payoff values refer to net cash flows over the two-year
period for each route through the tree.

The managing director then asked his colleagues if they could tell him which strategy he should follow in order to maximize his expected profit. Both the marketing manager and accountant felt that they could solve the one-year problem easily but they felt less sure about the two-year problem and were, therefore, keen to hire the services of a consultant decision analyst.

The managing director accepted the recommendation of his colleagues and authorized them to hire a consultant to help with the two-year problem. Before the meeting finished, however, the managing director asked the marketing manager and accountant to explain the solution to the short-run problem exhibited in Table 3.5. They agreed that *EMV* was a sensible decision rule and that, therefore, the Bayes strategy should be used to determine whether they should buy equipment or work existing plant on an overtime basis. They showed the managing director the *EMV* calculations in Table 3.5 which indicated that the overtime strategy was the most realistic strategy in *EMV* terms.

Their problem with the more long-range planning decision of two years was how to evaluate the optimal strategy. With a single-stage one-year decision they could see immediately that they must compare the S_1 and S_2 branches in terms of their *EMV* values. The logic of the solution to the one-year procedure that they proposed was to imagine themselves as being located at the extreme right-hand side of the one-year decision tree, where the monetary payoffs were. They then considered first the upper two branches of the tree with payoffs 220 and 130 and probabilities of 6 in 10 and 4 in 10 respectively of occurring. They argued that, if they moved back to the chance node from which the two branches emanated, they could calculate the *EMV* of being placed at that node, i.e. 184. Similarly, they could also calculate the *EMV* of being located at the lower chance node for the two lower branches of the tree, i.e. 186. The next step in the procedure was to imagine themselves as being transferred back to decision point 1 where they had the option of new equipment or overtime. Therefore, at decision point 1 they had the choice of selecting between two acts, S_1 and S_2, which each follow a route leading to a chance option whose expected profit (*EMV*) has already been calculated. The only rational choice at decision point 1 was to select S_2 which had the highest expected profit value. Thus, path S_1 was blocked off ($\wr\wr$) in the decision-tree diagram.

They thought that the same logic could be applied to the two-year diagram but were unsure of their ground. When the consultant arrived they put their problem to him and were reassured when he told them that their basic approach was correct. He said that XYZ's choice, i.e. the decision to invest in a new equipment or to settle for overtime working, involved a series of possible decisions in the future. The logic, therefore, is again to imagine yourself at the extreme right-hand side of the decision tree and try to transfer back to find the *EMV* for each of the six possible options emanating from decision point 2. By this means we can find the four optimal strategies at decision point 2 conditional upon the options available at decision point 1. Therefore, to evaluate the optimal strategy at decision point 1 you must imagine yourselves as being transferred to decision point 1 where you have the option of S_1 or S_2 whose *EMV*'s can now be calculated. The essence of this multi-stage solution procedure is that you *rollback* (or move back) the decision-tree diagram from the eighteen end-points with payoffs attached to one basic decision point and one preferred action or strategy. The rationale is that in making the decision at decision point 1, even though we are uncertain about its outcome, we must evaluate the alternative strategies with a consistent decision criterion such as *EMV* taking into account whatever circumstances and events may occur at any decision point, such as decision point 2, in the future.

In order to make sure that the reader can perform the rollback calculation and solution for the XYZ Company's two-year problem we reproduce in Tables 3.7 and 3.8 below the worksheets and final decision-tree diagrams produced by the marketing manager and the accountant.

TABLE 3.7

Worksheet Calculations for XYZ's Two-year Problem

(a) Analysis of decision point 2

Strategy (1)	Chance event (2)	Probability (3)	Payoff (4)	Expected payoff (*EMV*) (Col. 3 × Col. 4)
S_3	H	0·3	410	123·0
	M	0·3	395	118·5
	L	0·4	380	152·0
				Total 393·5
S_4	H	0·3	425	127·5
	M	0·3	408	122·4
	L	0·4	395	158·0
				Total 407·9

Note: S_4 is preferred to S_3 because of its higher *EMV*.

53

TABLE 3.7—(contd.)

Strategy (1)	Chance event (2)	Probability (3)	Payoff (4)	Expected payoff (*EMV*) (Col. 3 × Col. 4)
S_5	H	0·4	345	138·0
	M	0·4	325	130·0
	L	0·2	310	62·0
				Total 330·0
S_6	H	0·3	390	117·0
	M	0·3	360	108·0
	L	0·4	345	138·0
				Total 363·0
S_7	H	0·3	395	118·5
	M	0·3	370	111·0
	L	0·4	355	142·0
				Total 371·5

Note: S_7 is preferred to S_6 because of its higher *EMV*.

S_8	H	0·4	350	140·0
	M	0·4	335	134·0
	L	0·2	325	65·0
				Total 339·0

Note: After rollback to decision point 2 we are left with four expected payoffs, 407·9, 330·0, 371·5 and 339·0 which will be used in rolling back to decision point 1.

(b) *Analysis of decision point 1 in terms of expected monetary values*

Strategy (1)	Chance event (2)	Probability (3)	Cash flows (4)	Expected Value (Col. 3 × Col. 4)
S_1	R	0·6	407·9	244·7
S_1	F	0·4	330·0	132·0
				Total 376·7
S_2	R	0·6	371·5	222·9
S_2	F	0·4	339·0	135·6
				Total 358·5

We select S_1 because of its higher *EMV*.

It can be seen from Tables 3.7 and 3.8 that the optimal strategy in the two-year planning situation, i.e. invest in new equipment, differed from the overtime strategy which was optimal in the one-year case. In business terms it is easy to see why the conclusions differ in this way. On a short-term one-year basis overtime appears best because the investment cost is not fully matched by an immediate sales increase. In the longer term, i.e. the second year, the growth in sales volume makes up for the sales shortfall experienced in the first year. To some extent, therefore, the marketing manager and the accountant were justified in arguing for a long-run analysis in the executive committee's preliminary discussions of the capacity problem.

The unconvinced reader may say at this point that XYZ's decision problem was sufficiently simple that, given access to similar information sources as the decision-tree analysts, most decision-makers would have intuitively arrived at the decision to buy in new equipment. Whilst this may be true the value of a decision-tree approach should be clear. It enables attention to be focused on the main issues and uncertainties in the decision problem in a logical and structured manner.

Some decision-makers find it extremely difficult to transfer their decision problems into the logic of decision-tree diagrams. In most cases difficulties arise because of lack of experience and familiarity with tree diagrams and probabilistic concepts. We shall return to this point in the final chapter of this book and discuss there some of the issues that need to be resolved in order to make decision-tree analysis more acceptable to management.

For the moment, our position is that we have been through a highly simplified example of a multi-stage decision problem in terms of decision-tree analysis. Once you, as a decision-maker, are able to accept the structure implied by decision points, chance-event nodes, payoffs at the tips of the decision tree and the logic of the rollback calculation, you are ready to make use of decision-tree concepts. The problems which arise in the practical application of decision-tree concepts are those of detail rather than of logic. Though decision-tree concepts are themselves very simple, decision-tree diagrams which consider several alternatives and several chance events can quickly become very complicated.

For example in XYZ's problem the executive committee might have considered alternative strategies for reacting to the high demand for rev. counters. For example, XYZ could raise price in the short run which might attract competitive reaction by bringing in alternative suppliers. Or XYZ could argue that the high demand might be a temporary fluctuation and that a sensible short-term

Two-year Decision Tree for XYZ's Problem showing Rollback Evaluation of Optimal Strategy

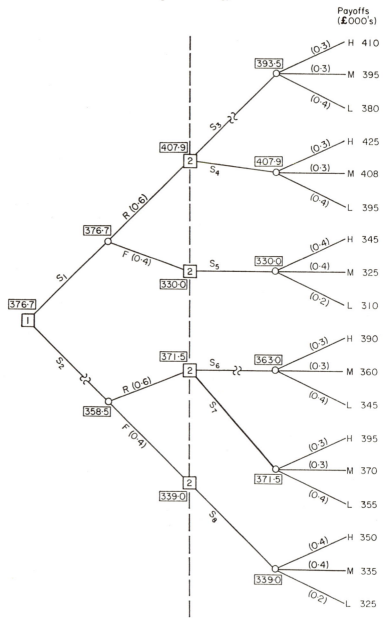

Payoffs
(£000's)

H	410
M	395
L	380
H	425
M	408
L	395
H	345
M	325
L	310
H	390
M	360
L	345
H	395
M	370
L	355
H	350
M	335
L	325

strategy might be to do nothing. Also the executive committee in XYZ considered only a limited range of sales levels, i.e. rise of 15 per cent in first year, fall of 5 per cent in first year and high, medium or low sales levels in the second year. It is perfectly possible, however, to extend the analysis to cover the whole range of probable price rises, falls and associated sales levels.

In later examples of applied decision analysis we shall demonstrate how decision-tree analysis can take account of added complexities in decision-tree diagrams. For the moment we must take up three further issues in the methodology of decision analysis:

(i) how the decision-maker should view future consequences against more immediate results;

(ii) whether the criterion of *EMV* adequately reflects the attitude of the decision-maker to the decision problem;

(iii) how to incorporate the results of further investigation or research into the decision-making and decision-tree analysis process.

These three issues can be illustrated briefly in terms of XYZ's problem. Realistically, net cash flows which occur in subsequent years of XYZ's planning problem do not have the same value as they would have if they occurred now. Logically, therefore, we must discount future net cash flows to their present values in order to be able to compare operationally cash flows which occur at different points in time in the planning period. In XYZ's case cash flows in the second year should be discounted at an appropriate rate of interest in order to compare them with cash flows accruing in the first year.

Valuing alternative strategies in terms of *EMV* is operationally valid if the decision-maker is indifferent between gain and loss in decision problems. However, since most decision-makers operate in the environment of firms and are accountable both for budgets and for their decisions to the managing director, they tend to avoid risk and adopt conservative attitudes. Because reward structures in

---

Notes to Table 3.8:

(i) The square boxes above chance nodes and decision points represent the *EMV*'s folded back of being at each node or decision point.

(ii) Rolling back from the 18 end-points to decision point 2 we block off (λ) strategies S_3 and S_6 on the basis of their smaller *EMV* values.

(iii) Rolling back from decision point 2 to decision point 1 we block off (λ) strategy S_2 because of its lower *EMV* value and choose S_1 as the optimal strategy.

firms tend to reward moderate success and severely penalize failure, managers operate conservatively and avoid risk in order to safeguard their careers. They are clearly not acting on the basis of *EMV* and their choice of the best strategy does not necessarily coincide with the company's best strategy. There is a need, therefore, for an alternative decision criterion to the expectation of monetary value. Earlier in this book it has been suggested that if we replace monetary value by a *utility* measure then expected utility should be the optimal decision criterion.

In XYZ's case the decision-maker might also decide to commission market research to find out through a survey about the expected demand patterns for revolution counters over the two-year period. Information collected in this way will change the initial probability assessments for sales presented in Table 3.8. We know from the chapter on basic ideas of probability theory that Bayes' theorem allows us to obtain revised probability assessments for sales levels in XYZ's case given information provided by the market-research firm.

In the next three sections we take up these three issues of *discounting*, *utility* and *revision of initial probability assessments* in terms of practical decision-tree analysis.

Discounting

It is important first of all to illustrate as simply as possible the application of the discounting concept as a means of accounting for the time value of money in a decision problem. Let us use once more the rev. counter capacity problem of firm XYZ. Suppose that we consider XYZ's two-year problem and that we assume for simplicity that the net cash flows for the two-year period are only discounted one year at the opportunity cost of capital for XYZ (roughly the rate which XYZ could earn by lending money on the open market), say 10 per cent. Operationally this means that the expected values at the tips of the one-year tree, i.e. 407·9, 330·0, 371·5 and 339·5 (see Table 3.8) have to be discounted by the factor $\dfrac{1}{1 + 0·1} = 0·909$ to give 370·8, 300·0, 337·7 and 308·6 respectively. Since the expected values have been discounted by the same factor, the analysis of the decision tree will still show S_1 to be the optimal strategy.

To make the discussion of discounting more meaningful, however, let us suppose that for XYZ certain net cash flows are incurred in year 1 and the remainder in year 2. If we assume first that the net cash flows generated in year 1 for XYZ are as in Table 3.9 (reproduced with alterations from Table 3.2),

TABLE 3.9

States of Nature

Strategy	R	F
S_1	220	130
S_2	210	150

then we can work out the cash flows along each of the points emanating from decision point 2, i.e. for the second year, as in the first three columns of Table 3.10.

TABLE 3.10

Cash Flows Emanating from Decision Point 2 (i.e. 2nd-year Cash Flows)

Strategy	Chance event	Cash flows in 2nd Year (Obtained as 2-year cash flows — 1-year cash flows)	Present value of cash flows at 10%
S_3	H	$410 - 220 = 190$	172·7
S_3	M	$395 - 220 = 175$	159·1
S_3	L	$380 - 220 = 160$	145·4
S_4	H	$425 - 220 = 205$	186·3
S_4	M	$408 - 220 = 188$	170·9
S_4	L	$395 - 220 = 175$	159·1
S_5	H	$345 - 130 = 215$	195·4
S_5	M	$325 - 130 = 195$	177·2
S_5	L	$310 - 130 = 180$	163·6
S_6	H	$390 - 210 = 180$	163·6
S_6	M	$360 - 210 = 150$	136·3
S_6	L	$345 - 210 = 135$	122·7
S_7	H	$395 - 210 = 185$	168·2
S_7	M	$370 - 210 = 160$	145·4
S_7	L	$355 - 210 = 145$	131·8
S_8	H	$350 - 150 = 200$	181·8
S_8	M	$335 - 150 = 185$	168·2
S_8	L	$325 - 150 = 175$	159·1

The fourth column in the Table presents the cash flows for the second year (these are assumed to accrue as a lump sum at the end of the second year for purposes of calculation) discounted at 10 per cent (i.e. by a factor $\dfrac{1}{1 + 0·1} = 0·909$) to give present value equivalents at the end of year 1 (i.e. at decision point 2).

We are in a position now to analyse decision point 2 with discounting, i.e. to evaluate the first stage of the rollback procedure. The analysis is presented in Table 3.11.

Having rollbacked to decision point 2 we should now carry out the second stage and rollback to decision point 1. For simplicity, we shall assume that the first-year cash flow is not discounted (any reader who is sufficiently interested can do the calculations easily by multiplying end of year one cash flows by the factor $\dfrac{1}{1 + 0\cdot1} = 0\cdot909$).

TABLE 3.11

Obtaining Discounted Expected Values at Decision Point 2

Strategy	Chance event	Probability	Present value	Discounted expected present value
S_3	H	0·3	172·7	$(0\cdot3 \times 172\cdot7) + (0\cdot3 \times 159\cdot1)$
	M	0·3	159·1	$+(0\cdot4 \times 145\cdot4)$
	L	0·4	145·4	$= 51\cdot8 + 47\cdot7 + 58\cdot2$
				$= 157\cdot7$
S_4	H	0·3	186·3	$(0\cdot3 \times 186\cdot3) + (0\cdot3 \times 170\cdot9)$
	M	0·3	170·9	$+ (0\cdot4 \times 159\cdot1)$
	L	0·4	159·1	$= 55\cdot9 + 51\cdot3 + 63\cdot6$
				$= 170\cdot8$
S_5	H	0·4	195·4	$(0\cdot4 \times 195\cdot4) + (0\cdot4 \times 177\cdot2)$
	M	0·4	177·2	$+ (0\cdot2 \times 163\cdot6)$
	L	0·2	163·6	$= 78\cdot2 + 70\cdot9 + 32\cdot7$
				$= 181\cdot8$
S_6	H	0·3	163·6	$(0\cdot3 \times 163\cdot6) + (0\cdot3 \times 136\cdot3)$
	M	0·3	136·3	$+ (0\cdot4 \times 122\cdot7)$
	L	0·4	122·7	$= 49\cdot1 + 40\cdot9 + 49\cdot1$
				$= 139\cdot1$
S_7	H	0·3	168·2	$(0\cdot3 \times 168\cdot2) + (0\cdot3 \times 145\cdot4)$
	M	0·3	145·4	$+ (0\cdot4 \times 131\cdot8)$
	L	0·4	131·8	$= 50\cdot5 + 43\cdot6 + 52\cdot7$
				$= 146\cdot8$
S_8	H	0·4	181·8	$(0\cdot4 \times 181\cdot8) + (0\cdot4 \times 168\cdot2)$
	M	0·4	168·2	$+ (0\cdot2 \times 159\cdot1)$
	L	0·2	159·1	$= 72\cdot7 + 67\cdot3 + 31\cdot8$
				$= 171\cdot8$

Note: S_4 is preferred to S_3.⎫ In both cases because of more favourable
$\quad\quad\;\; S_7$ is preferred to S_6.⎭ EMV figures.

Table 3.12 presents the analysis of the decision problem viewed from decision point 1.

TABLE 3.12

Analysis of Decision Point 1

Strategy	Chance event	Probability	Cash flow	EMV
S_1	R	0·6	220 + (from decision 170·8 point 2) ——— 390·8	0.6×390.8 $+ 0.4 \times 311.8$ $= 234.5 + 124.7$ $= 359.2$
S_1	F	0·4	——— 130 + (from decision 181·8 point 2) ——— 311·8	
S_2	R	0·6	210 + (from decision 146·8 point 2) ——— 356·8	0.6×356.8 $+ 0.4 \times 321.8$ $= 214.1 + 128.7$ $= 342.8$
S_2	F	0·4	——— 150 + (from decision 171·8 point 2) ——— 321·8	

Note: On the EMV analysis S_1 is the preferred strategy.

The revised decision tree for the discounting situation is presented in Table 3.13.

The reader should now at least understand the meaning of discounting even if he is not able to perform the calculations adequately. Money has a time value and £1 now is worth more to me than £1 a year hence because I could have earned 5 per cent, say, by investing the money in a building society account. Similarly, money received by XYZ in year 2 is not the same as money received in year 1 because of this interest element, the time value of money. Logically, therefore, to make cash flows strictly comparable we must discount cash flows received in year 2 to their equivalent value in year 1. In this sense discounting is the inverse of compounding.

Any reader who has had his appetite for discounting mathematics whetted should refer to Merrett and Sykes[3] for fuller details.

TABLE 3.13

Payoffs
(2nd year
cash flows)

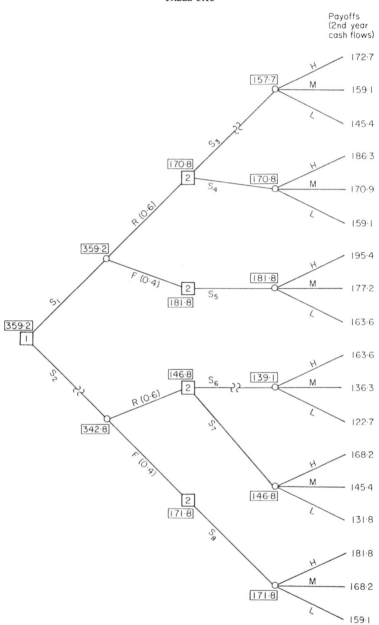

Note: discounting is only performed on the second-year cash flows.

Utility

In the analysis of XYZ's decision problem we have obtained the optimal strategy by calculating the *EMV* criterion. There are at least two situations in business where *EMV* is not likely to be a valid criterion. First, if the decision-maker finds difficulty in expressing the values of some of the outcomes of his decisions as monetary payoffs, *EMV* cannot be used. An example of such a situation might be the monetary valuation of siting the third London airport at Cublington, Thurleigh or Foulness. Elements of a monetary valuation in such a situation are environmental and social factors which cannot objectively be assessed in monetary terms. This should be apparent from the post-Roskill debate which waged for several months in the British press and journals.

Second, however, *EMV* breaks down most often because it assumes that the individual decision-maker is indifferent to risk. Earlier, we noted that decision-makers in general act to avoid risk, particularly if there is any possibility whatsoever of incurring a loss. There is, therefore, some value in finding another measure which describes better how the decision-maker values possible outcomes.

The decision-theory literature suggests that utility is a relevant measure for the value of an outcome. To illustrate its meaning we return to the other problem that has been introduced in our previous discussion, viz. the problem of which investment strategy to adopt if you are uncertain about the state of the economy. The basic structure of the problem is reproduced again in Table 3.14.

TABLE 3.14

Mr Z's Yield (%) for Various Investment Strategies conditional upon the State of the Economy

Probabilities	State of Economy		
	$(\frac{1}{3})$	$(\frac{1}{3})$	$(\frac{1}{3})$
Strategy	Growth	Stagnation	Decline
a_1	20	1	-6
a_2	10	6	0
a_3	4	4	4

This example has been chosen because the yield can become negative (i.e. a loss can be made) if the wrong strategy, for example a_1, is adopted. In our earlier discussion we saw that alternative criteria such as *Maximin* can reflect a pessimistic attitude on the part of the decision-maker. Utility is a measure which ranks the decision-maker's preferences for the attainment of the nine possible yields in the investment uncertainty situation depicted above.

To illustrate how to obtain the investor's utility function let us first arbitrarily assign a utility of 1 utile to the best possible outcome, 20 per cent, and a utility of 0 utiles to the worst possible outcome, −6 per cent. The other seven yield values will then have utility values between 0 and 1. We shall obtain the utility for the yield value of 10 per cent to illustrate the method and leave the reader to work out how utility values can be obtained in the other six cases.

The decision-maker would clearly like the utility measure to describe his relative rankings between yield values. One way of doing this is to ask the decision-maker to visualize a hypothetical gambling situation in which he can obtain 20 per cent, the best yield, with probability P and −6 per cent, the worst yield, with probability $1 - P$. The decision-maker is told that 10 per cent can be obtained with certainty. He is then asked to tell the analyst the value of P, the probability of getting a 20 per cent yield, which would make him just indifferent between getting 10 per cent for certain or a gamble with probability P of getting 20 per cent and $1 - P$ of getting −6 per cent (i.e. he would take either the gamble or 10 per cent for certain at that level of P). Suppose that the decision-maker assigns P a value of 0·7 after a period of contemplation. Given this assignment we can now find the utility value for a yield of 10 per cent, i.e. U (10 per cent) as follows:

$$U(10 \text{ per cent}) = PU(20 \text{ per cent}) + (1 - P)U(-6 \text{ per cent})$$
$$= (0·7 \times 1) + (0·3 \times 0)$$
$$= 0·7 \text{ utiles}$$

This calculation merely repeats in mathematical terms the fact that the decision-maker would be indifferent between 10 per cent for certain and a gamble with $\frac{7}{10}$ probability of getting 20 per cent.

Similarly, by the use of further hypothetical gambling situations we could obtain the utility values for the other six yields. Table 3.15 shows a graph of the utility function for the investor.

From this rough graph we can obtain utility values for the investor's problem as shown in Table 3.16.

For this problem we can now compare the *EMV* and expected utility strategies using the information contained in Tables 3.14 and 3.16. The *EMV* strategy calculations follow first:

64

TABLE 3.15
Investor's Utility Function

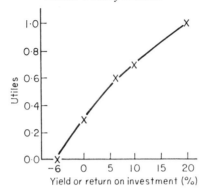

Yield (%)	Utiles
20	1·0
10	0·7
6	0·6
0	0·3
−6	0·0

TABLE 3.16
Utility Values for Investor's Problem

Probabilities	$(\frac{1}{3})$	$(\frac{1}{3})$	$(\frac{1}{3})$
Strategy	Growth	Stagnation	Decline
a_1	1·0	0·35	0·0
a_2	0·7	0·6	0·3
a_3	0·5	0·5	0·5

$EMV(a_1) = 5$, $EMV(a_2) = 5\frac{1}{3}$, $EMV(a_3) = 4$ (from Table 3.2).
The EUV (expected utility) calculations are obtained similar by;

$EUV(a_1) = (\frac{1}{3} \times 1\cdot0) + (\frac{1}{3} \times 0\cdot35) + (\frac{1}{3} \times 0\cdot0) = \underline{\underline{0\cdot45}}$ utiles

$EUV(a_2) = (\frac{1}{3} \times 0\cdot7) + (\frac{1}{3} \times 0\cdot6) + (\frac{1}{3} \times 0\cdot3) = \underline{\underline{0\cdot53}}$ utiles

$EUV(a_3) = (\frac{1}{3} \times 0\cdot5) + (\frac{1}{3} \times 0\cdot5) + (\frac{1}{3} \times 0\cdot5) = \underline{\underline{0\cdot5}}$ utiles

Thus EMV and EUV both select a_2 as the optimal strategy, though
the a_1 and a_3 strategies are valued differently under the two criteria.

In this illustrative example, therefore, the investor's objective can be adequately, expressed by the maximization of *EMV* since the maximization of *EUV* leads to the same optimal strategy.

Whilst the theoretical value of the utility concept is apparent there is a long way to go before it is efficiently implemented. Grayson[4] reported in his studies of the oil and gas exploration process that investors, i.e. oil wildcatters, were willing to accept the relevance of *EMV* or profit but not *EUV*. Quite apart from the scepticism expressed by decision-makers there are still severe measurement problems to be overcome in obtaining utility functions and in resolving issues of whether utility functions remain stable over time. At the moment, therefore, we suggest that *EMV* is the most operationally realistic criterion and we shall not try here to throw any further light on the utility concept.

Revision of Probabilities

Suppose that we consider one possible information-gathering option available to the decision-maker in the XYZ Company. For the purposes of illustration we shall only treat the one-year decision problem of XYZ, i.e. deciding whether to buy new equipment or run the existing plant on an overtime basis, in termss of the decision-maker's prior assessments of a sales rise or fall in the market. The decision-tree for this case has already been exhibited in Table 3.5 and so we will merely reproduce the final decision tree in Table 3.17 without further discussion.

TABLE 3.17

Prior Analysis of XYZ's Decision Tree

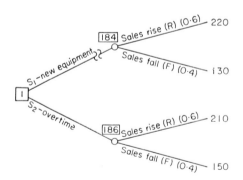

Note: Prior analysis suggests that S_2—the overtime strategy—is the optimal strategy.

The decision-maker in XYZ, however, does not feel happy about making a decision on the basis of this prior analysis. He wants some confirmation that his subjective probabilities of 0·6 for a sales rise and 0·4 for a sales fall are a reliable set of assessments for sales. After discussions with the managing director he decides that he should call up their market-research adviser. The adviser consults with a number of market-research firms and concludes that he should recommend a survey which will give an indication of the correct state of the market, i.e. a sales *rise* or *fall* in the first year, with 80 per cent reliability. The decision-maker accepts the marketing adviser's recommendations after hearing that 80 per cent reliability is a reasonable compromise to accept from a market-research investigation. 100 per cent reliability can never be achieved in market research because of the problems of measurement and sampling error.

The decision-maker then instructs the market-research company to carry out a survey, at a cost of £5,000, which will indicate one of two things, either that a sales rise or a sales fall is the correct state of the market. The decision-maker then asks the decision analyst to explain how he should make use of the survey information. The analyst proceeds to set down the calculations involved and the associated decision tree as shown in Table 3.18.

In Table 3.18 the analysis of the purchase survey option is carried out using the now familiar *rollback* principle to evaluate the expected monetary value as of decision point 1. The immediate conclusion that can be made after undertaking this analysis is that the *net* expected payoff if the survey option is undertaken is 184·2. This is less than the expected value of 186·0 obtained by the decision-maker from his prior analysis of XYZ's decision problem (see Table 3.17). In operational terms this means that the cost of the survey, £5,000, exceeds the gain, £189,200−£186,000 = £3,200, to be expected from carrying out the survey. Clearly it is a waste of money to contemplate a £5,000 survey in this situation because £3,200 must be the *maximum* amount that the decision-maker should spend on an 80 per cent reliable survey. Any cost exceeding £3,200 would be uneconomical. If some other market-research firm offered an 80 per cent reliable survey at a cost less than or at most equal to £3,200 then the decision-maker should accept the offer because he would gain in expected payoff terms from the receipt of survey information.

The analysis of the survey option in this situation at least forces a decision-maker, such as XYZ's, to recognize how much he should spend on information-gathering activities, such as market-research surveys.

TABLE 3.18

Worksheet Calculations and Decision Tree for the Survey Option

---

Notation

1. Assume that the survey yields only two results, Z_1 and Z_2. Z_1 indicates that a sales rise (R) is the correct state and Z_2 indicates that a sales fall (F) is the correct state.

2. This means that the appropriate *conditional probabilities* are given as follows (because we have an 80 per cent reliable survey):

$P(Z_1/R) = 0.8$

$P(Z_2/F) = 0.8$

$P(Z_1/F) = 0.2$

$P(Z_2/R) = 0.2$

3. The *prior* probabilities of a sales rise (R), $P(R)$ and sales fall, $P(F)$ are $P(R) = 0.6$, $P(F) = 0.4$.

4. We want to find the revised probability assessments for sales rise and sales fall given the evidence of the survey, i.e. $P(R/Z_1)$, $P(R/Z_2)$, $P(F/Z_1)$ and $P(F/Z_2)$ respectively.

Bayes' theorem, discussed in the probability chapter, is the mechanism by which we shall obtain these revised probability assessments. The formulae for these revised probability assessments are given below:

$$P(R/Z_1) = \frac{P(R)\,P(Z_1/R)}{P(R)\,P(Z_1/R) + P(F)\,P(Z_1/F)}$$

$$= \frac{0.6 \times 0.8}{(0.6 \times 0.8) + (0.4 \times 0.2)} = 0.86$$

$$P(R/Z_2) = \frac{P(R)\,P(Z_2/R)}{P(R)\,P(Z_2/R) + P(F)\,P(Z_2/F)}$$

$$= \frac{0.6 \times 0.2}{(0.6 \times 0.2) + (0.4 \times 0.8)} = 0.27$$

$$P(F/Z_1) = \frac{P(F)\,P(Z_1/F)}{P(F)\,P(Z_1/F) + P(R)\,P(Z_1/R)}$$

$$= \frac{0.4 \times 0.2}{(0.4 \times 0.2) + (0.6 \times 0.8)} = 0.14$$

$$P(F/Z_2) = \frac{P(F)\,P(Z_2/F)}{P(F)\,P(Z_2/F) + P(R)\,P(Z_2/R)}$$

$$= \frac{0.4 \times 0.8}{(0.4 \times 0.8) + (0.6 \times 0.2)} = 0.73$$

5. In addition, we need to find the *marginal* probabilities with which events Z_1 and Z_2 occur from the survey.

$$P(Z_1) = P(R)\,P(Z_1/R) + P(F)\,P(Z_1/F)$$

$$= (0.6 \times 0.8) + (0.4 \times 0.2)$$

$$= 0.56$$

$$P(Z_2) = P(R)\,P(Z_2/R) + P(F)\,P(Z_2/F)$$

$$= (0.6 \times 0.2) + (0.4 \times 0.8)$$

$$= 0.44$$

6. We can now draw the decision tree associated with the *survey option*.

TABLE 3.18—*(cont.)*

Worksheet Calculations and Decision Tree for the Survey Option—(cont.)

DECISION TREE

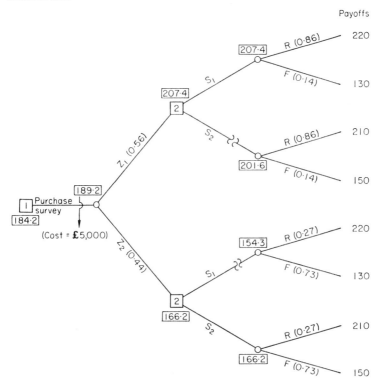

ANALYSIS OF DECISION TREE

(a) *Analysis of Decision Point 2*

	Strategy (1)	Chance event (2)	Probability (3)	Payoff (4)	Expected payoff (Col. 3 × Col. 4)	
Upper branch emanating from Z_1	S_1	R	0·86	220		189·2
		F	0·14	130		18·2
					Total	207·4
	S_2	R	0·86	210		180·6
		F	0·14	150		21·0
					Total	201·6

On basis of expected payoff (*EMV*), S_1 is selected.

TABLE 3.18—(cont.)

ANALYSIS OF DECISION TREE—*Analysis of Decision Point 2—(cont.)*

	Strategy (1)	Chance event (2)	Proba-bility (3)	Payoff (4)	Expected payoff (Col. 3 × Col. 4)
Lower branch emanating from Z_2	S_1	R F	0·27 0·73	220 130	59·4 94·9
					Total 154·3
	S_2	R F	0·27 0·73	210 150	56·7 109·5
					Total 166·2

On basis of expected payoff (*EMV*), S_2 is selected.

(b) *Analysis of Decision Point 1*

	Strategy (1)	Chance event (2)	Proba-bility (3)	Payoff (4)	Expected payoff (Col. 3 × Col. 4)
Purchase Survey		Z_1 Z_2	0·56 0·44	207·4 166·2	116·1 73·1
					Total 189·2
			Less cost of survey		5·0
					184·2

Therefore *EMV* of the purchase survey strategy is 184·2.

The full decision analysis, incorporating the prior analysis (i.e. no-sampling option) and the sampling options, for XYZ's decision-maker is shown in Table 3.19.

This decision analysis has illustrated how Bayes' theorem should be used to revise the decision-maker's *prior* probability assessments of 0·6 and 0·4 for a sales rise and fall respectively, in the light of survey evidence. The only difference between this decision-tree analysis and earlier ones is that additional information could be obtained by the decision-maker. The same principle, *rollback*, has been used to evaluate the optimal strategy once the decision tree has been drawn and all payoff valuations and probability assessments have been obtained.

In subsequent chapters we shall apply the same mode of analysis to a typical set of business-decision problems.

TABLE 3.19

Full Decision Tree for XYZ's Information-gathering Situation

Payoffs

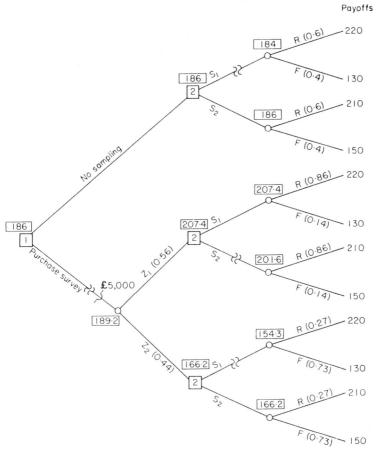

SUMMARY AND REVIEW

This chapter discusses the fundamentals of the decision-tree concept and shows how they apply to the analysis of decision problems. The next chapter (or section) of this book applies the decision-tree analysis method developed by this stage to a number of business-decision problems. Thus, by indicating how the method applies to a wide range of problems we hope to encourage the reader to use decision-analysis concepts in helping to clarify his own particular decision problems. The input for our subsequent discussion is, thus, an understanding and appreciation of decision-tree concepts. Since more complex multi-stage decision trees are essentially built up from simple one-stage decisions we repeat in Table 3.20 below a simple decision tree for a situation in which there are two alternative decisions (a_1 and a_2) and three chance events, E_1, E_2, and E_3, which affect each possible decision. The outcome or payoff of taking any decision will depend upon the combination of the decision with the set of possible chance events.

TABLE 3.20

Simple One-stage Decision Tree

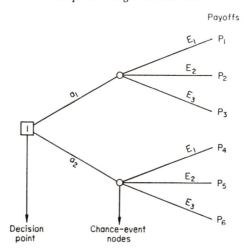

In order to choose between a_1 and a_2 four main tasks must be completed. First, the structure of the decision tree must be evaluated and drawn. Second, the chance events which affect the decision must be identified and probabilities assessed for the occurrence of these chance events. Third, values to be attached to the six possible payoffs, P_1, P_2, ... P_6 must be estimated. Fourth, a criterion, *EMV*, must be used as the standard of value which discriminates between alternative decision paths and allows the optimal decision strategy to be evaluated.

The four stages involved in analysing a decision tree apply to multi-stage, sequential decision problems as well as the single-stage decision depicted in Table 3.20. The reader should refer back

72

to the XYZ example (starts at Table 3.5) to confirm his understanding of the decision-tree concept.

Review of Essential Concepts

A number of concepts must be understood before the reader proceeds to the case-study section:

(i) THE IDENTIFICATION OF THE DECISION PROBLEM AND ITS DECOMPOSITION INTO DECISION-TREE LAYOUT

In the summary we have outlined the four main steps which must be carried out in order to analyse a decision tree. The crucial steps, however, are those in which the structure of the tree is developed. Decomposing a decision problem, once it has been identified, into the form of a decision tree is the most difficult and complex stage of a decision analysis: which alternatives should the decision-maker consider? What chance events, *a priori*, are likely to affect the alternatives? What future decisions or options might the decision-maker be faced with over the planning period considered?

The three questions itemized are the main ones which the decision-maker has to resolve in the task of transferring his decision problem into an equivalent decision-tree representation. This task is commonly referred to as the *decomposition* problem in decision analysis. If the decomposition of the decision problem is satisfactory then the subsequent analysis of the decision tree is likely to be useful to the decision-maker. A decomposition accomplished without careful thought and consideration is likely to be bad and the subsequent analysis in this situation should not be carried out until the decision-maker has adequate faith in the logic and correctness of the decision tree.

(ii) THE APPROPRIATE STANDARD OF VALUE, CHOICE CRITERION, FOR BUSINESS DECISION-MAKING

The appropriate choice criterion for discriminating between alternative strategies is the expected-profit (EMV) criterion where profit should be expressed, via discounting concepts, in present-value terms. Alternative choice criteria based on minimax or Hurwicz criteria should *never* be used unless the decision-maker feels unable to specify a probability distribution for the chance events (or states of nature). Even when the decision-maker's probability assignments are vague and uncertain they should be regarded as his reflection of the weightings which should be attached to the uncertain events. This approach is to be preferred to arbitrary criteria which suggest that you are always going to get the *best* or the *worst* outcome. These criteria are themselves making specific assumptions about the probability distribution on the uncertain events which cannot always be justified in relation to the decision-maker's degrees of belief about those events however uncertain and vague those degrees of belief may be.

A few comments need also to be made about the *utility* concept. We introduced the idea of the utility of money earlier in Chapter 2 in terms of a hypothetical gamble which argued that significant increases in money wealth are worth less than decreases of the same size to many gamblers. To take another example, the XYZ Company might invest £20,000 in a new rev. counter machine with a 0·5 probability of producing either £60,000 or £0 (i.e. $EMV = £30,000$). If, however, it has to decide whether to invest £20 million in machinery with a 0·5 probability of getting either £60 million or £0 ($EMV = £30$ million) it might be very wary especially if any loss would mean that the firm would become insolvent.

Over and above this demonstration that a company might prefer to avoid loss when the money "threshold" invested rises, there are other reasons which make the utility concept appealing. In particular, because of the divorce of owner from manager, the utility of a financial gain from an investment may be quite different to the departmental manager than to the firm as a corporate entity.

Despite the intuitive attractions of the utility concept, it has not been widely implemented in practice because of measurement difficulties and managerial scepticism. For these reasons, we suggest that the *EMV* criterion should be used as the choice criterion in business decision-making, pending the development of more operationally useful and acceptable utility measurement procedures.

(iii) THE ROLLBACK PRINCIPLE

This is the basic principle by means of which we can analyse a complex multi-stage decision tree (see, for example, XYZ's problem in the text). We first imagine ourselves as being transported out to the tips of the decision tree, where the payoffs are given for the problem. We then work our way backwards to the initial decision point by means of two procedures:

(i) averaging out at each chance event node;
(ii) choosing at each decision point the path that yields the maximum future payoff.

The reader should review the worked example, i.e. the XYZ case, before proceeding to the analysis of further cases.

(iv) ALLOWANCE FOR THE TIME VALUE OF MONEY IN DECISION-TREE ANALYSIS

The reader should review the section on discounting techniques which explains how to obtain present-value equivalents for cash flows accruing in future years of the life of a business investment.

(v) ESTIMATION OF PROBABILITIES, CASH FLOWS AND THE RELEVANT DISCOUNT RATE FOR THE INVESTMENT-DECISION PROBLEM

(a) *Probabilities* of uncertain quantities such as sales may be estimated objectively from a statistical analysis of sales patterns obtained from past data or market-research information. Alternatively, the decision-maker may have to assign subjective probabilities to sales which reflect his degrees of belief about sales patterns. The assessment of subjective probabilities requires careful analysis and thought on the part of the decision-maker.

(b) *Cash flows and payoffs* are typically estimated by integrating the information from the marketing, production and accounting departments and other relevant functional areas.

(c) *The discount rate* should be chosen as the interest rate which the firm would require from an investment characterized by roughly the same level of uncertainty.

(vi) THE INTEGRATION OF INFORMATION AND EVIDENCE TO REVISE PRIOR PROBABILITIES IN DECISION ANALYSIS

One valid option for a decision-maker in many business decision problems is the collection of further research or information before making a decision. This does not imply time-wasting tactics on the part of the decision-maker but may reflect a desire for a further look at the problem or a need for confirmation of prior feelings and beliefs.

The XYZ Company problem was used to show the value of an information-gathering option for the XYZ Company. The calculations showed how the revision of the decision-maker's prior assessments is obtained by incorporating the sample evidence with the prior assessments in terms of Bayes' theorem.

References

1. Williams, B. R., and Scott, W. P., *Investment Proposals and Decisions*, Allen & Unwin, 1965.
2. Raiffa, H., *Decision Analysis*, Addison-Wesley, 1968.
3. Merrett, A. J., and Sykes, Allen, *The Finance and Analysis of Capital Projects*, Longmans, 1965.
4. Grayson, C. J., Jr., *Decisions under Uncertainty—Drilling Decisions by Oil and Gas Operators*, Division of Research, Harvard Business School, Boston, 1960.

PART II

Applications of
Decision Analysis

4   *Case Studies*

In the previous three chapters we have discussed the basic foundations of decision analysis, viz. probability (Chapter 1), the nature of decision problems (Chapter 2), and decision trees (Chapter 3).

In this chapter we extend this discussion by illustrating the application of these concepts to a number of business problems. We have already considered one application because in the decision-tree chapter we followed through the decision-tree analysis for the new-plant decision problem of the XYZ Company. This type of new-plant decision problem is a common investment-decision problem in industry and readers should, therefore, study the XYZ Company's problem in as much detail as the other case studies.

The choice of the "case studies" presented here has been determined through the author's knowledge of business problems in which decision-analysis concepts have been effectively applied in operational terms. For reasons of clarity and simplicity, however, we have made the case studies of manageable proportions and have not tried to model all the uncertainties and alternatives that may exist in such situations.

Four case studies are evaluated and they cover the following problem areas:

   (i) new product decisions;
  (ii) oil and gas exploration decisions;
 (iii) research and development decisions;
 (iv) pricing decisions.

The first three problems are examples of investment decisions at the firm level whilst the fourth is a problem of price-setting in a competitive market.

NEW-PRODUCT DECISIONS

New-product planning is an important part of business planning in the modern-day environment. This is because competition between firms in a market is more often carried out through the introduction of new products rather than through price manipulation. Even so, there are risks involved in marketing new products. There is always the possibility of failure in launching the new product and this risk can be as high as 1 in 5 in markets where technological change is endemic.

The use of decision trees in new-product planning forces the marketing manager to structure the decision processes involved in launching the new product. This process of problem-structuring in turn will help him, for example, to determine whether it is worth while to collect some market-research data on a test-market basis before carrying out a broad-scale national launch.

We will illustrate the application of decision-tree analysis to new-product decisions in terms of a number of simple problems. These problems should help the marketing man to understand how to draw decision trees for marketing problems and to recognize options and branches on the tree which are unfavourable to the attainment of his overall objective which may, for example, be to maximize and increase his market-share position.

CASE A

Launching a New Product

The C.S. Company has developed a new instant potato product which will enter a market in which there are already a number of alternative brands. Preliminary consumer-taste testing of the pilot output indicates that consumer reaction to the product is likely to be favourable. The marketing manager has to decide whether the product should be launched nationally immediately. His alternative strategies are either to carry out further test marketing by launching in a small region of the country first or to scrub the new product entirely. Obviously if a national launch were undertaken the firm would incur significant investment expenditure on the purchase of further machinery and plant. The more cautious small regional launch would not require immediate expenditure on new equipment because the pilot plant would be able to handle the maximum expected demand levels for instant potato within the sales test region.

The production manager estimated that the investment costs for new equipment for the national launch would be £200,000 including all installation charges. Present marketing information based on taste testing and subjective hunch indicates that three alternative forecasts of potential sales, given the national launch, should cover the possible levels of future sales. The marketing staff have also come to a consensus about the subjective probabilities that should be assigned to the likelihood of occurrence of each forecast level. For each possible forecast level of sales the marketing and accounting staff have been able to calculate the payoffs for a national launch because the price of instant potato is effectively determined (and is therefore a certain quantity) by the prices of alternative brands. Table 4.1 summarizes the information available for the *national launch* strategy.

TABLE 4.1

Payoff Matrix for National Launch Strategy
(Payoff—in Net Present-value Terms)

	States of nature		
	$P(\theta_1) = 0\cdot2$ θ_1 High Sales	$P(\theta_2) = 0\cdot6$ θ_2 Medium Sales	$P(\theta_3) = 0\cdot2$ θ_3 Low Sales
Launch the product	£1,000,000	£200,000	−£500,000
Do not launch	0	0	0

In the oversimplified decision problem set out in Table 4.1, the decision-maker should calculate the *EMV* for each strategy and fold back to obtain the optimal strategy under the prior analysis. This is shown very clearly in the decision tree exhibited in Table 4.2.

The prior analysis indicates that the marketing decision-maker should launch the new product on the basis of the existing information. Since, however, he and his colleagues were a bit wary about launching solely on the basis of prior information, they decided to consider delaying their decision pending the collection of additional data which would throw further light upon the probabilities of occurrence of high, medium or low sales levels. The trade-offs for collecting information to refine initial probability assessments are the costs involved in collecting the information, the resulting delay in launching the new product and the impossibility of ever getting perfectly reliable data about sales levels.

The marketing staff felt that they would need one year to launch the product on a limited regional basis and collect 80 per cent reliable

TABLE 4.2

Decision Tree for the Prior Analysis of the Product Launch

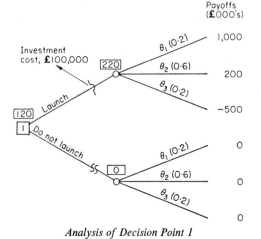

Analysis of Decision Point 1

Strategy (1)	Chance event (2)	Probability (3)	Payoff (4)	Expected payoff (Col. 3 × Col. 4)
*LAUNCH	θ_1	0·2	1,000	200
	θ_2	0·6	200	120
	θ_3	0·2	−500	−100
			Total	220
			Less Investment Cost	100
			NET	120
ABANDON				0

(* denotes optimal strategy)

data about ultimate sales levels. The costs of the test marketing exercise were estimated to be £5,000. In addition, the payoffs to be expected over the planning horizon would be reduced from the levels in Table 4.1 because of the discount penalty for delay (i.e. money is received one year later instead of right now) and the potential effect of delay on the firm's share of the instant potato market. A rough reduction of 10 per cent across the board was thought to be a reasonable reflection of the costs of delay.

The marketing staff then sat down with the decision analyst and drew the decision tree for the test-marketing option in one region.

They decided that they had the choice of three possible strategies after they had received the test-marketing information: first, to launch on a national basis; second, to restyle the product if low sales are indicated at an approximate cost of £10,000 ready for either a national launch or a complete *stop* one year later; third, to scrub the product entirely. The decision tree for the one-year delay option is shown in Table 4.3.

TABLE 4.3

Worksheet Calculations and Decision Tree for One-year Delay Option

WORKSHEET CALCULATIONS

Note:

1. The prior probabilities of high, medium and low sales were 0·2, 0·6 and 0·2 respectively.

2. The test market indicates either z_1, i.e. high sales (H) will occur
or z_2, i.e. medium sales (M) will occur
or z_3, i.e. low sales (L) will occur.

Because the test market is only 80 per cent reliable, $P(z_1/H) = 0·8$,
$$P(z_2/M) = 0·8,$$
and $P(z_3/L) = 0·8$
and also $P(z_1/M) = P(z_1/L) = P(z_2/H) = P(z_2/L) = P(z_3/H) = P(z_3/M)$
$= 0·1$

3. Therefore, $P(z_1) = P(z_1/H)P(H) + P(z_1/M)P(M) + P(z_1/L)P(L)$
$= (0·8 \times 0·2) + (0·1 \times 0·6) + (0·1 \times 0·2) = \underline{0·24}$

$P(z_2) = P(z_2/H)P(H) + P(z_2/M)P(M) + P(z_2/L)P(L) = (0·1 \times 0·2)$
$+ (0·8 \times 0·6) + (0·1 \times 0·2) = \underline{0·52}$

$P(z_3) = P(z_3/H)P(H) + P(z_3/M) P(M) + P(z_3/L)P(L) = (0·1 \times 0·2)$
$+ (0·1 \times 0·6) + (0·8 \times 0·2) = \underline{0·24}$

4. We need the revised probabilities of high, medium or low demand *after* the test market indications, i.e. we need $P(H/z_1)$, etc.

$$P(H/z_1) = \frac{P(H)P(z_1/H)}{P(z_1)} = \frac{0·2 \times 0·8}{0·24} = \underline{0·67};$$

$$P(H/z_2) = \frac{P(H)P(z_2/H)}{P(z_2)} = \frac{0·2 \times 0·1}{0·52} = \underline{0·04};$$

$$P(H/z_3) = \frac{P(H)P(z_3/H)}{P(z_3)} = \frac{0·2 \times 0·1}{0·24} = \underline{0·08};$$

TABLE 4.3—(*cont.*)

$$P(M/z_1) = \frac{P(M)P(z_1/M)}{P(z_1)} = \frac{0 \cdot 6 \times 0 \cdot 1}{0 \cdot 24} = \underline{\underline{0 \cdot 25}};$$

$$P(M/z_2) = \frac{P(M)P(z_2/M)}{P(z_2)} = \frac{0 \cdot 6 \times 0 \cdot 8}{0 \cdot 52} = \underline{\underline{0 \cdot 92}};$$

$$P(M/z_3) = \frac{P(M)P(z_3/M)}{P(z_3)} = \frac{0 \cdot 6 \times 0 \cdot 1}{0 \cdot 24} = \underline{\underline{0 \cdot 25}};$$

$$P(L/z_1) = \frac{P(L)P(z_1/L)}{P(z_1)} = \frac{0 \cdot 2 \times 0 \cdot 1}{0 \cdot 24} = \underline{\underline{0 \cdot 08}};$$

$$P(L/z_2) = \frac{P(L)P(z_2/L)}{P(z_2)} = \frac{0 \cdot 2 \times 0 \cdot 1}{0 \cdot 52} = \underline{\underline{0 \cdot 04}};$$

$$P(L/z_3) = \frac{P(L)P(z_3/L)}{P(z_3)} = \frac{0 \cdot 2 \times 0 \cdot 8}{0 \cdot 24} = \underline{\underline{0 \cdot 67}}.$$

5. The probabilities for high, medium and low sales after the product had been restyled were assessed to be 0·1, 0·6 and 0·3 respectively. The payoffs after restyling make allowance for the delay in launching the product on to the market.

6. *Analysis of Decision Tree for One Year Delay Option*

(*a*) *Analysis of Decision Point 3*

(*Indicates optimal strategy)

Strategy (1)	Chance event (2)	Proba-bility (3)	Payoff (£ thousand) (4)	Expected payoff (*EMV*) (Col. 3 × Col. 4)
National launch	H	0·1	800	80
	M	0·6	160	96
	L	0·3	−400	−120
			Total	56
			Less: Investment cost	− 82
			Net	− 26
*Stop				− 15

DECISION TREE

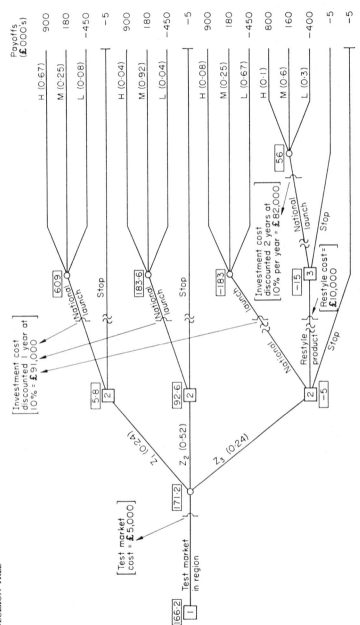

Payoffs
(£000's)

TABLE 4.3—(cont.)

(b) Analysis of Decision Point 2
(*Indicates optimal strategy)

Strategy (1)	Chance event (2)	Probability (3)	Payoff (4)	Expected payoff (Col. 3 × Col. 4)	
Upper Branch					
*National launch	H	0·67	900		600
	M	0·25	180		45
	L	0·08	−450		−36
				Total	609
				Less: Investment cost	−91
					518
Stop					−5
Middle Branch					
*National launch	H	0·04	900		36
	M	0·92	180		165·6
	L	0·04	−450		−18·0
				Total	183·6
				Less: Investment cost	−91·0
				Net	92·6
Stop					−5
Low Branch					
National launch	H	0·08	900		72
	M	0·25	180		45
	L	0·67	−450		−300
				Total	−183
				Less: Investment cost	−91
					−274
Restyle product					−15
				(from earlier analysis of Dec. Pt. 3)	
				Less: Restyle costs	−10
					−25
*Stop					−5

TABLE 4.3—(cont.)

(c) *Analysis of Decision Point 1*

Strategy (1)	Chance event (2)	Proba- bility (3)	Payoff (4)	Expected payoff (Col. 3 × Col. 4)	
Test Market	z_1	0·24	518		124·3
	z_2	0·52	92·6		48·1
	z_3	0·24	−5		−1·2
				Total	171·2
				Less: Test market cost	−5·0
				Net	166·2

The process of averaging out and folding back (i.e. rolling back) the decision tree in Table 4.3 shows that the test-market delay option has an *EMV* of £166,400 which exceeds the prior analysis *EMV*, i.e. immediate launch, by £46,400. This suggests that the correct decision in this new-product launch situation should be to test market and launch the product only if the test market indicates *high* or *medium* sales.

Obviously, in the tree in Table 4.3 we could consider delaying the launch for periods greater than one year, e.g. two years, three years and so on. The effect of delay would be to increase the reliability of the information obtained from the test market at the expense of greater survey—i.e. test marketing—costs and further delays in launching the product (thus forgoing immediate returns and incurring possible losses in market share). Nevertheless, the structure we have outlined would allow the marketing staff to investigate in a logical and formal manner the two-year delay option and any other possible information-gathering strategy.

Perhaps the next interesting feature of the new-product analysis is that it confirms one of the commonly held beliefs in marketing theory, i.e. that test marketing is of value in a new-product launch situation. Whilst test marketing is useful in the case we have analysed there will be situations where changed circumstances and expectations about sales will indicate that information-gathering activities such as test marketing convey no extra gain in terms of *EMV*. In those changed circumstances the firm should obviously launch the product as quickly as possible.

It would clearly be valuable to extend the framework we have developed in order to answer the question of how, and in what terms, the decision-maker should place a value on market research. If he is offered a survey by a market-research company he must have a mechanism in order to evaluate formally how much the information is worth to him. It is always true that information helps decision-making but if the expected gain from having the information is less than the expected cost of getting it the decision-maker should not bother collecting the information.

We shall illustrate the value of information concepts in Case B.

CASE B

The Valuation of Market-Research Survey Information

A firm, ABC Ltd, has developed a new product and after some preliminary consumer studies the marketing director reviews the situation by making some estimates of profit and loss resulting from the achievement of market-share levels of 10 per cent, 3 per cent and 1 per cent respectively. Table 4.4 presents the results of the marketing director's appraisal. The costs involved in scrubbing the product are given as zero, on the argument that development costs for the new product are sunk and are not relevant for current decision-making.

TABLE 4.4

Payoff Matrix for ABC's New Product Launch
(Payoffs in £ thousand) (discounted)

Acts	States of nature (Sales levels)		
	$P(\theta_1) = 0.7$ $\theta_1 = 10\%$	$P(\theta_2) = 0.1$ $\theta_2 = 3\%$	$P(\theta_3) = 0.2$ $\theta_3 = 1\%$
Launch product	100	20	−60
Scrub product	0	0	0

Note: Prior analysis gives,
$$EMV \text{ (launch)} = (100 \times 0.7) + (20 \times 0.1) - (60 \times 0.2)$$
$$= 60$$

$$EMV \text{ (scrub)} = 0$$

Therefore, we should always launch on the basis of the prior analysis.

Now, after prior analysis, the important question is whether it is worth while to collect some additional market-research information to throw further light upon the probability assessments for the states of nature before taking the final decision. The way to determine the benefits of research is to compare the expected value of what appears to be the optimal act after research less the cost of the research with the expected value of the apparently best act before research. If the net gain after research is positive, then the market-research information is economically worth while.

To help set limits on the value of the research, it is useful to consider what would happen if we had "perfect information". We can think of the *expected profit under certainty* as that which we would realize if we were to take the best action for each state of nature that actually materializes. Thus, where market shares of 10 per cent and 3 per cent would be forecast, the optimal act would be to introduce the new product; whereas if a 1 per cent market share were forecast, the optimal act would be to scrub the product. In other words, if the probabilities given as subjective in Table 4.4 were thought of as being based on relative frequencies, the expected value of the optimal act under conditions of perfect certainty would be $(0 \cdot 7 \times 100) + (0 \cdot 1 \times 20) + (0 \cdot 2 \times 0) = 72$.

The £12,000 difference between the expected value of the optimal act under conditions of perfect certainty and that of the optimal act before any research (based on our subjective probabilities) is called the *expected value of perfect information* (*EVPI*). This sets the maximum limit on the value obtainable through market research and immediately rules out spending more than £12,000, even for a research project which will predict subsequent results perfectly.

By introducing the concept of perfect certainty, therefore, we have obtained an *upper limit or bound*, £12,000, for any expenditure on market-research information.

Suppose that a specific MR proposal for £1,000 is offered to the marketing manager. This proposal offers the option of either test marketing the product or collecting information from consumer panels. After some thought, the test-marketing option seems more favourable because it can be done extremely quickly and the manager sets out to evaluate the worth of this particular proposal. His basic rule is that the gain in expected value of the optimal act after the research over that prevailing before the research must be at least equal to the cost of that research.

The market-research company tells him that the test market will indicate either a market share of 10 per cent (z_1) or a market share of 3 per cent (z_2) or a market share of 1 per cent (z_3). z_1 and z_2 will be indicated with 60 per cent reliability whereas z_3 will be indicated with 80 per cent reliability. The full set of conditional probabilities for the test-market outcomes is given in Table 4.5.

TABLE 4.5

Conditional Probabilities of Possible Test Market Outcomes given Three Sales
Levels for a New Product

Sales level	Test market indication		
	z_1	z_2	z_3
θ_1	0·6	0·3	0·1
θ_2	0·3	0·6	0·1
θ_3	0·1	0·1	0·8

Next, the marketing manager must try to combine the conditional probabilities of the test-market results with the original prior estimates of the probabilities of sales levels (or "states of nature") to revise the probabilities to be attached to the various levels θ_1, θ_2 and θ_3. Obviously, Bayes' theorem is the mechanism we should use to revise the initial probability assessments for the sales levels. The purpose of carrying out the research is to enable a *posterior analysis* of these probabilities to be undertaken because the marketing manager wants to find out something about the future market share achieved by the new product rather than to measure the test-market results for its own sake.

In Table 4.6 we exhibit the Bayes' theorem calculations for the posterior probability assessments $P(\theta/z)$, where the θ's refer to the states of nature (sales levels) and the z's to the test-market results.

With the revised probability assessments we can now formally analyse the expected value of the option to test market the product before the final launch. This, in terms of the now familiar decision-tree concept is shown in Table 4.7.

As a result of the analysis using the averaging out and foldback principle it can be seen that the expected value of introducing the new product after a market test would be £61·6 thousand pounds. This would mean a net gain in expected value terms of (61·6 − 60) thousand pounds, i.e. £1,600, over the option of introducing the product immediately on the basis of the prior assessments on the various possible sales or market-share levels.

We can formalize the verbal analysis we have just made and define the *Expected Net Gain of Sample (Test Market) Information (ENGSI)* as the *Expected Value of Sample (Test Market) Information (EVSI)* minus *Cost of Sample (Test Market) Information*. The *EVSI* is the difference between the expected value of the optimal strategy after the test market exclusive of survey costs, i.e. £62·6 thousand, minus the expected value of the optimal strategy on the prior analysis,

TABLE 4.6

Bayes' Theorem Calculations for Revised Probabilities of Future Sales Levels

(a) *Probabilities for various test market results: z_1, z_2 and z_3*

$$
\begin{aligned}
P(z_1) &= P(z_1/\theta_1)P(\theta_1) + P(z_1/\theta_2)P(\theta_2) + P(z_1/\theta_3)P(\theta_3) \\
&= (0{\cdot}6 \times 0{\cdot}7) \;\; + (0{\cdot}3 \times 0{\cdot}1) \;\; + (0{\cdot}1 \times 0{\cdot}2) \\
&= 0{\cdot}42 \qquad\quad + 0{\cdot}03 \qquad\quad + 0{\cdot}02 \\
&= 0{\cdot}47
\end{aligned}
$$

$$
\begin{aligned}
P(z_2) &= P(z_2/\theta_1)P(\theta_1) + P(z_2/\theta_2)P(\theta_2) + P(z_2/\theta_3)P(\theta_3) \\
&= (0{\cdot}3 \times 0{\cdot}7) \;\; + (0{\cdot}6 \times 0{\cdot}1) \;\; + (0{\cdot}1 \times 0{\cdot}2) \\
&= 0{\cdot}21 \qquad\quad + 0{\cdot}06 \qquad\quad + 0{\cdot}02 \\
&= 0{\cdot}29
\end{aligned}
$$

$$
\begin{aligned}
P(z_3) &= P(z_3/\theta_1)P(\theta_1) + P(z_3/\theta_2)P(\theta_2) + P(z_3/\theta_3)P(\theta_3) \\
&= (0{\cdot}1 \times 0{\cdot}7) \;\; + (0{\cdot}1 \times 0{\cdot}1) \;\; + (0{\cdot}8 \times 0{\cdot}2) \\
&= 0{\cdot}07 \qquad\quad + 0{\cdot}01 \qquad\quad + 0{\cdot}16 \\
&= 0{\cdot}24
\end{aligned}
$$

(b) *Revised probabilities for the market share levels*

$$
P(\theta_1/z_1) = \frac{P(\theta_1)P(z_1/\theta_1)}{P(z_1)} = \frac{0{\cdot}7 \times 0{\cdot}6}{0{\cdot}47} = 0{\cdot}90
$$

$$
P(\theta_1/z_2) = \frac{P(\theta_1)P(z_2/\theta_1)}{P(z_2)} = \frac{0{\cdot}7 \times 0{\cdot}3}{0{\cdot}29} = 0{\cdot}72
$$

$$
P(\theta_1/z_3) = \frac{P(\theta_1)P(z_3/\theta_1)}{P(z_3)} = \frac{0{\cdot}7 \times 0{\cdot}1}{0{\cdot}24} = 0{\cdot}29
$$

$$
P(\theta_2/z_1) = \frac{P(\theta_2)P(z_1/\theta_2)}{P(z_1)} = \frac{0{\cdot}1 \times 0{\cdot}3}{0{\cdot}47} = 0{\cdot}06
$$

$$
P(\theta_2/z_2) = \frac{P(\theta_2)P(z_2/\theta_2)}{P(z_2)} = \frac{0{\cdot}1 \times 0{\cdot}6}{0{\cdot}29} = 0{\cdot}21
$$

$$
P(\theta_2/z_3) = \frac{P(\theta_2)P(z_3/\theta_2)}{P(z_3)} = \frac{0{\cdot}1 \times 0{\cdot}1}{0{\cdot}24} = 0{\cdot}04
$$

$$
P(\theta_3/z_1) = \frac{P(\theta_3)P(z_1/\theta_3)}{P(z_1)} = \frac{0{\cdot}2 \times 0{\cdot}1}{0{\cdot}47} = 0{\cdot}04
$$

$$
P(\theta_3/z_2) = \frac{P(\theta_3)P(z_2/\theta_3)}{P(z_2)} = \frac{0{\cdot}2 \times 0{\cdot}1}{0{\cdot}29} = 0{\cdot}07
$$

$$
P(\theta_3/z_3) = \frac{P(\theta_3)P(z_3/\theta_3)}{P(z_3)} = \frac{0{\cdot}2 \times 0{\cdot}8}{0{\cdot}24} = 0{\cdot}67
$$

TABLE 4.7
Decision Tree for the Test Market Option

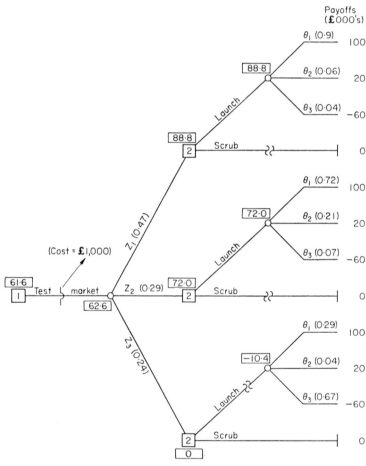

Payoffs
(£000's)

θ_1 (0·9)	100
θ_2 (0·06)	20
θ_3 (0·04)	−60

88·8 — Launch

88·8 / 2 — Scrub — 0

θ_1 (0·72) — 100
θ_2 (0·21) — 20
θ_3 (0·07) — −60

72·0 — Launch

Z_1 (0·47)

(Cost = £1,000)

61·6 / 1 — Test / market — 62·6

Z_2 (0·29) — 72·0 / 2 — Scrub — 0

Z_3 (0·24)

θ_1 (0·29) — 100
θ_2 (0·04) — 20
θ_3 (0·67) — −60

−10·4 — Launch

2 / 0 — Scrub — 0

92

TABLE 4.7—(*cont.*)

Analysis of the Test Market Decision Tree
(a) *Analysis of Decision Point 2*
(*Denotes Optimal Strategy)

Strategy (1)	Chance event (2)	Proba-bility (3)	Payoff (£ thousand) (4)	Expected payoff (Col. 3 × Col. 4)	
Upper Branch *Launch	θ_1	0·90	100		90
	θ_2	0·06	20		1·2
	θ_3	0·04	−60		−2·4
				Total	88·8
Scrub					0
Middle Branch *Launch	θ_1	0·72	100		72·0
	θ_2	0·21	20		4·2
	θ_3	0·07	−60		−4·2
				Total	72·0
Scrub					0
Lower Branch Launch	θ_1	0·29	100		29·0
	θ_2	0·04	20		0·8
	θ_3	0·67	−60		−40·2
					−10·4
*Scrub					0

(b) *Analysis of Decision Point 1*
(*Denotes Optimal Strategy)

Strategy (1)	Chance event (2)	Proba-bility (3)	Payoff (£ thousand) (4)	Expected payoff (Col. 3 × Col. 4)	
Test market	z_1	0·47	88·8		41·7
	z_2	0·29	72·0		20·9
	z_3	0·24	0		0
				Total	62·6
				Less: Test market cost	−1·0
					61·6

i.e. £60 thousand. This gives a value of £2·6 thousand to the *EVSI* in this case. Since the test-market option costs £1 thousand, *ENGSI* = (£2·6 − £1) thousand = £1·6 thousand.

In operational terms the *ENGSI* concept is saying that it would pay us to spend up to £2·6 thousand (i.e. the level at which *ENGSI* would be zero) in order to confirm the judgements about the probabilities of various market-share levels. Any sum in excess of £2·6 thousand for a test-market survey would be uneconomical and valueless.

This particular test-market survey has obviously been of great benefit to the decision-maker. The £12,000 limit on the value obtainable through market research has now been reduced to £12,000 − £2,600 = £9,400 after the test-marketing exercise. If any further information-gathering were contemplated by the marketing manager after test marketing, £9,400 would be the new *upper limit* on any further information-gathering expenditure.

One word of caution is opportune after this discussion of the method for valuing potential information from market-research investigations. The concepts *of net gain from sample information* and *value of sample information* have been formulated in terms of expected values. A particular survey commissioned by a marketing manager may prove to be more or less reliable than expected before the research is carried out. The revised probabilities on the market-share levels may, therefore, be different in a particular case and this will affect the monetary amounts that we shall gain from carrying out the survey in this particular case. This means that *actual* values for the gain from sample information will generally differ from those expected initially. Nevertheless, the concepts of *EVSI* and *ENGSI* provide the marketing manager with the best economic indications of the worth of various possible survey options before any experimentation is carried out. They give *average* limits for the net *gain* and *value* to be expected from survey information. Thus, the marketing manager has guidelines which enable him to analyse the *a priori* worth of particular information-gathering programmes which are offered to him. Acceptance of options is made in terms of an economic criterion of expected net gain rather than, for example, by a "seat of the pants" approach of collecting information because some market-research firm has offered you a survey.

OIL AND GAS EXPLORATION DECISIONS

Decision-tree analysis concepts have been most widely applied in the area of oil and gas exploration. Studies by Grayson[1] and Kaufman[2] at the Harvard Business School have laid down the framework of the decision problem faced by typical oil and gas operators in exploring various sites for further oil and gas wells.

For our purposes we shall take an illustrative and simplified example of an oil-exploration decision problem. Suppose that an oil explorer, commonly called a wildcatter, must decide whether to drill a well or sell his rights in a particular exploration site. The desirability of drilling depends upon whether there is oil beneath the surface. Before drilling, the wildcatter has the option of taking seismographic readings which will give him further geological and geophysical information. This information will enable him to deduce whether subsurface structures usually associated with oil fields exist in this particular location. However, some uncertainty about the presence of oil will still exist after seismic testing because oil is sometimes found where no subsurface structure is detected and vice versa.

In order to make a rational decision the wildcatter must find out about the various options open to him. First he must determine how much he would get if he sold his rights in the exploration site immediately. Second, he must evaluate the financial prospects if oil is recovered from the site. Third, he must formalize his uncertainties about the chance events which affect his decision-making in terms of *odds* or probability assessments about their occurrence. For example, what is the probability that a well in which subsurface structure is found will nevertheless produce no oil?

After much discussion with his accountant and engineers, the wildcatter estimates that the cost of drilling a well on this site would be £90,000 in net present-value terms after making allowance for all taxes. The yield that would be expected from a typical oil well is estimated to be £400,000 in net present-value terms, net of all taxes and operating costs but excluding drilling costs.

Seismic tests would cost £10,000 per test and would be expected to give an indication of the existence of subsurface structure.

The wildcatter feels that, should he decide to sell the site before either drilling or testing it, he could sell his rights for £50,000. However, if he should decide to carry out seismographic readings and no subsurface structure is indicated, the site will be considered worthless by other wildcatters and he could gain nothing from the sale of the rights for the site at that stage.

Having set down the monetary values expected from each of the options, the wildcatter reviews his feelings about the probabilities of getting oil from the site. He assigns prior probabilities of 0·4 and 0·6 to the probabilities of striking an oil well or a dry well. If he carries out the seismic test he feels that the test will indicate subsurface structure with 50 per cent probability. In addition, he makes assessments for the probabilities of "structure and oil", "structure and no oil", "no structure and oil" and "no structure and no oil" as shown in Table 4.8 on the basis of past drilling experience in oilfields.

TABLE 4.8

| Test Reveals | State of Well | | |
	Oil	Dry	
Structure	0·3	0·2	0·5
No Structure	0·1	0·4	0·5
	0·4	0·6	

It can easily be seen from this table that the probability of oil given structure must be given by the ratio $\frac{0\cdot3}{0\cdot5} = 0\cdot6$. Intuitively this says that the probability of oil given subsurface structure is the ratio of the joint probability of "subsurface structure and oil" to the probability of subsurface structure. This is really no different from the usual form in which we present Bayes' theorem. Bayes' theorem as we have developed it so far formally states that

$$\text{Probability (Oil/Structure)} = \frac{P(\text{Oil})P(\text{Structure/Oil})}{P(\text{Structure})} \quad (1)$$

$$\text{where } P(\text{Structure}) = P(\text{Structure/Oil})P(\text{Oil}) + P(\text{Structure/Dry})P(\text{Dry}) \quad (2)$$

Now the numerator of expression (1), i.e. $P(\text{Oil}) \times P(\text{Structure/Oil})$ can be assessed either by getting the probability of oil and multiplying by the probability of structure given oil or by getting the *joint* probability of "structure and oil" directly. This is because the probability of "structure and oil" is identically equal to the product of the probability of oil and the probability of structure given oil (a little reflection from the reader and a review of the probability chapter presented earlier should ensure that this statement can be verified quite easily).

In Table 4.9 we give the values for the revised probabilities of striking oil after the seismic test.

Having analysed the financial outcomes for the options open to him and assigned probabilities for the various events which affect his decision-making, the oil wildcatter is now in a position to analyse his problem by the decision-tree analysis.

The structure of his decision tree is shown in Table 4.10 and the analysis is given in Table 4.11.

TABLE 4.9

Revised Probabilities of Oil and Dry Wells after Seismic Test

(a) P(Oil/Test reveals Structure)

$$= \frac{P(\text{Oil and Structure})}{P(\text{Structure})} = \frac{0 \cdot 3}{0 \cdot 5} = \underline{\underline{0 \cdot 6}}$$

(b) P(Dry/Test reveals Structure)

$$= \frac{P(\text{Dry and Structure})}{P(\text{Structure})} = \frac{0 \cdot 2}{0 \cdot 5} = \underline{\underline{0 \cdot 4}}$$

(c) P(Oil/Test reveals No Structure)

$$= \frac{P(\text{Oil and No Structure})}{P(\text{No Structure})} = \frac{0 \cdot 1}{0 \cdot 5} = \underline{\underline{0 \cdot 2}}$$

(d) P(Dry/Test reveals No Structure)

$$= \frac{P(\text{Dry and No Structure})}{P(\text{No Structure})} = \frac{0 \cdot 4}{0 \cdot 5} = \underline{\underline{0 \cdot 8}}$$

TABLE 4.10
Decision Tree for the Oil Wildcatter

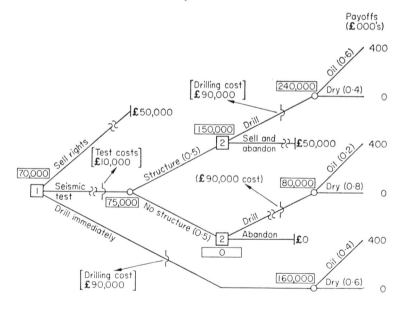

TABLE 4.11

Analysis of the Wildcatter's Decision Tree

(a) *Analysis of Decision Point 2* (*Denotes optimal strategy)

Strategy (1)	Chance event (2)	Proba-bility (3)	Payoff (£1 thousand) (4)	Expected value (*EMV*) (5) (Col. 3 × Col. 4)	
Upper branch *Drill	Oil	0·6	400		240
	Dry	0·4	0		0
				Total	240
				Less: drilling cost	90
				Net	150
SELL AND ABANDON					50
Lower branch Drill	Oil	0·2	400		80
	Dry	0·8	0		0
				Total	80
				Less: drilling cost	90
				Net	−10
*ABANDON					0

By averaging out and folding back we can see that the wildcatter's optimal strategy, if we accept *EMV* as a decision criterion, should be to drill the well immediately. The *EMV* of this strategy, i.e. £70,000, is £5,000 greater than the *EMV* for the seismic-test option. In this situation, despite the collection of seismographic readings, the prior-analysis option of drilling immediately turns out to be better. Different sets of probability assessments might change the optimal strategy but the present analysis at least shows that sample information, i.e. seismic testing, does not always have to be collected.

The wildcatter's decision problem may be more complex than the simple one presented here. The site may have both oil and natural-gas wells. The effect of this on the decision tree would be to increase the 2-position chance event branches for oil or dry wells to a 4-position branch, i.e. either an oil or a gas well or both an oil and a

TABLE 4.11—(cont.)

(b) *Analysis of Decision Point 1* (*Denotes optimal strategy)

Strategy (1)	Chance event (2)	Proba-bility (3)	Payoff (£ thousand) (4)	Expected value (EMV) (5) (Col. 3 × Col. 4)	
Sell rights					50
Seismic test	Structure	0·5	150		75
	No Structure	0·5	0		0
				Total	75
				Less: Cost of Seismic Test	10
					65
*Drill immediately	Oil	0·4	400		160
	Dry	0·6	0		0
				Total	160
				Less: drilling cost	90
					70

gas well or neither (dry). The addition of these two extra branches would force the decision-maker to make additional probability assessments for "gas" and "both oil and gas" and necessitate the valuation of productive gas wells as well as productive oil wells.

If the wildcatter suspects both oil and gas wells to be present on the site, then he must also refine his seismic-testing procedures. Subsurface formations which indicate oil and gas will tend to be different and this would suggest that additional branches for the test results should be added to the decision tree. A rough decision-tree structure, without *EMV* analysis, for this more complex situation is shown in Table 4.12.

We will not formally analyse the more complex tree shown above or make the necessary monetary valuations and probability assessments. Such valuations and assessments can easily be made by the decision-maker once he understands and accepts the formal structure of his decision problem as shown by his decision tree. The crucial step in any case analysis that the reader may carry out himself is the process of drawing the decision tree. Once the rationality of the decision tree is recognized the assessments of probabilities for chance events and monetary valuations for outcomes can be made in a much more meaningful fashion.

TABLE 4.12

Decision-tree Structure if Wildcatter's Site May Have Both Oil and Gas

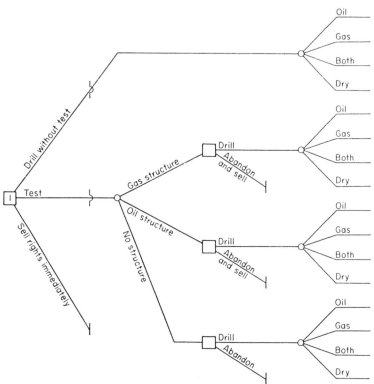

RESEARCH AND DEVELOPMENT DECISIONS

Peck[3], in an article on the role of technology and science in the British economy, suggests that R & D project decisions made in British industry do not take adequate account of production cost and marketing considerations. In simple terms Peck argues that a major reason for the lack of success of British products is that the management of R & D activities is far weaker than that in the United States. Whilst the management of R & D in the US is probably based on sounder economic considerations and an ability to commercialize technical ideas quickly, there is evidence (see Peck and

100

Scherer[4], Meadows[5]) that the management of R & D exhibits similar weaknesses in terms of cost overruns and inadequate definition of the final market.

For all of these reasons a great deal of effort is being directed towards the development of methods which will help the R & D manager to appraise the worth of projects which are generated with his R & D activity. Research and Development spending can be looked upon as an investment and evaluated in the same manner as other investment opportunities. If an R & D decision is an investment decision then a financial criterion is a reasonable criterion for analysing the worth of particular projects.

Let us suppose that the executives of HPE Ltd regard R & D decisions as investment decisions and are faced with a decision about a project to develop a series of sophisticated electronic measurement instruments. Although the measurement instruments will give the firm a competitive edge the R & D manager has doubts about the firm's technical capability in this new area of electronic measurement. The marketing and sales engineers are pushing him hard, however, because they feel that there will be a huge market demand for the instrument if it can be developed and launched within two years. Under the circumstances the R & D manager feels that the firm has a 50/50 chance of completing the development within the two-year period. If the two-year period has to be exceeded the firm will lose money because of incurring extra development costs and losing the opportunity of establishing a strong initial market hold.

The R & D manager has been to some lectures given by a consultant on the subject of decision trees and thinks that they could usefully be applied to the problem of getting a worth assessment for the instrument project. He sets down a rough draft of the decision tree as shown in Table 4.13.

Certain features of this rough draft need elaboration. First, the decision maker (R & D manager) has assumed a five-year sales life for the product and a two-year development period. This is thought to be in line with the views of the marketing staff though different diagrams could be drawn for other product life-cycle patterns. Second, the whole of the diagram has not been drawn out because the decision-maker quickly realized that the simple decision tree that he was hoping to draw was becoming a "bushy mess" in need of some immediate remedial pruning. The number of chance events considered (i.e. uncertainties in the project's investment cost, final price and sales levels) quite apart from the number of possible strategies, required the assessment of too many probabilities and the valuation of too many end-points in the decision tree.

The R & D manager decided to consult with his project engineers

101

TABLE 4.13
R & D Manager's Rough Draft of Decision Tree

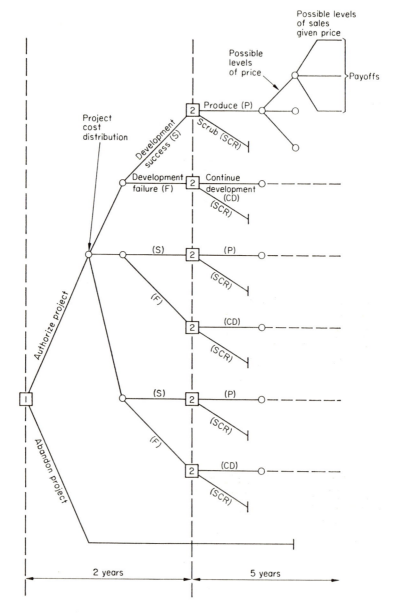

TABLE 4.14 *Amended Decision Tree for the Instrument R & D Project*

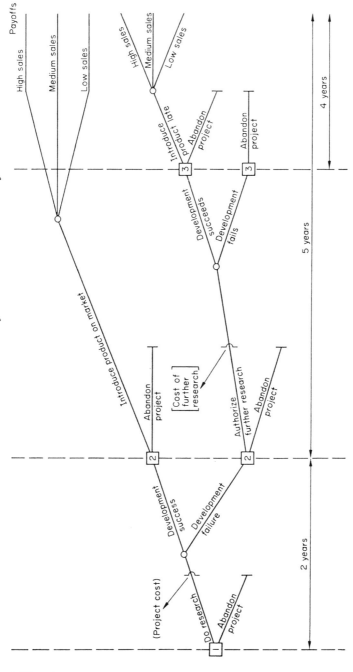

and after some discussion he came up with an amended and simple version of the decision tree.

This decision tree assumes that project cost and price can be estimated with reasonable certainty. The R & D manager feels that he can put forward a strong case to justify the firm's price for the product being estimated very accurately because the number of competitors is small, i.e. the market is oligopolistic (few suppliers) on the supply side. Although cost estimation in this firm is not always very accurate, the project engineers have assured the R & D manager that the cost figure given is the maximum conceivable figure. If the project looks good on this cost basis then it should be undertaken because we are looking at the largest possible cost that the engineers feel will happen, i.e. the extreme point on the probability distribution for cost.

The R & D manager then sat down with his project engineers to estimate the probabilities and monetary valuations necessary for the analysis of the decision tree—working outwards from the initial decision they worked out the maximum cost for the research as being £40,000. Despite protests from a few project engineers the R & D manager felt that the consensus view was that there was a 50/50 chance of completing the development successfully in two years. If the development was a failure they felt that they might be able to authorize a further sum of £20,000 (in present-value terms) to enable the research team to complete the development work within the next year. The chances of successfully completing the development work in a further year were assessed at a 30/70 chance on the group view that technical uncertainties uncovered in the first two years would make the task of the research team in "tying up loose ends" that bit more difficult in the third year of development. They felt that the project should be abandoned if the development work did not turn out a viable working instrument in three years because competitive instruments would be nearing market launch by that time and would reduce the market share which HPE could expect. On the other hand, if they had a product ready to launch at the end of three years the group assessed a 1/10 chance of getting a discounted payoff (in terms of contribution—net of all taxes and operating costs) of £120,000, a 5/10 chance of getting a discounted payoff of £60,000 and a 4/10 chance of getting a discounted payoff of £30,000.

They felt that their payoff prospects would be much better if they could get the product on to the market in two years. In those circumstances, they assessed a 2/10 chance of a discounted payoff of £160,000, a 5/10 chance of a discounted payoff of £80,000 and a 3/10 chance of a discounted payoff of £40,000.

Finally, if they had to abandon the project at *any* time they would

104

not count as losses any inroads that competitors might make through introduction of a similar product.

With this information they proceeded to draw the final decision tree and work out whether or not they should proceed with the development work on the instrument. The decision tree together with the associated analysis is presented in Table 4.15.

TABLE 4.15

Analysis of Decision Tree for HPE Ltd's Instrument Project

(a) Decision Tree Diagram

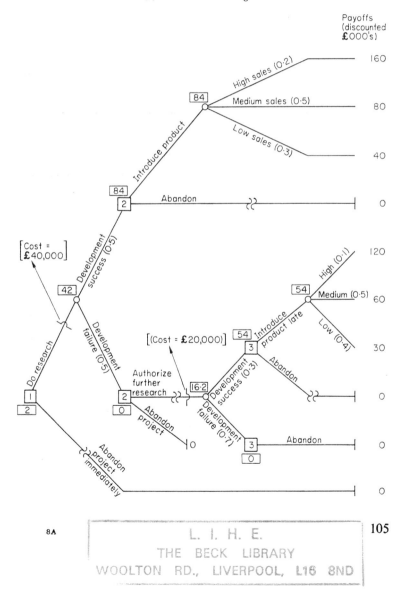

TABLE 4.15—(cont.)

(b) *Analysis of Decision-tree Diagram*

(i) *Analysis of Decision Point 3* (*Denotes optimal strategy)

Strategy (1)	Chance event (2)	Proba-bility (3)	Payoff (£ thousand) (4)	Expected payoff (Col. 3 × Col. 4)	
*Introduce product late	High sales	0·1	120		12
	Medium sales	0·5	60		30
	Low sales	0·4	30		12
				Total	54
Abandon after Success					0
Abandon after Failure					0

(ii) *Analysis of Decision Point 2* (*Denotes optimal strategy)

Strategy (1)	Chance event (2)	Proba-bility (3)	Payoff (£ thousand) (4)	Expected payoff (Col. 3 × Col. 4)	
Upper branch *Introduce product	High sales	0·2	160		32
	Medium sales	0·5	80		40
	Low sales	0·3	40		12
				Total	84
Abandon					0
Lower branch Authorize research	Dev success	0·3	54		16·2
	Dev failure	0·7	0		0
				Total	16·2
				Less: Research cost	20·0
				Net	−3·8
*Abandon					0

TABLE 4.15—(*cont.*)

(iii) *Analysis of Decision Point 1* (*Denotes optimal strategy)

Strategy (1)	Chance event (2)	Probability (3)	Payoff (£ thousand) (4)	Expected payoff (Col. 3 × Col. 4)	
Upper branch					
*Do research	Dev success	0·5	84		42
	Dev failure	0·5	0		0
					—
				Total	42
				Less: Cost of	
				Research	40
					—
				Net	2
					=
Lower branch					
Abandon					0
					=

The optimal strategy, in terms of the *EMV* criterion, is to do the research and introduce the product if the development is successful after two years but abandon the project if the development work fails in the two-year period.

The *EMV* of the optimal strategy in present-value payoff terms is £2,000. This value should be compared with the *EMV*'s of other possible projects before research is authorized and commenced. Of course, the *EMV* figure is an expected figure and in practical terms it only gives a guideline for the *actual* gain that may accrue to the firm. If the £40,000 research cost is large in relation to the firm's financial resources, then it may be realistic to use expected *utility* rather than *EMV* as the decision criterion. This would, in turn, require measuring the decision-maker's (i.e. the R & D manager's) utility function for money as we did for Mr Z's investment problem in Chapter 3.

In summary, this case shows that decision-tree concepts can be applied to the R & D decision. More complex analyses incorporating additional strategies and chance events could have been presented, but such analyses are best carried out in terms of the R & D problems of particular firms. Our aim has been to present a simplified structure for the logical analysis of R & D decisions.

PRICING DECISIONS

The decision-tree procedure can also be employed in the process of setting a price for a new product. We shall show how the concept might be used in relation to a case problem of price-setting in an imperfectly competitive market. Other concepts based on economic theory suggest price policies which managers can adopt in imperfectly competitive situations (see Dean[6], for example). What we hope to show is that the decision-tree method provides a structure and a set of guidelines for a manager to follow in determining a pricing policy. We expect that decision trees will be used by more and more managers because they allow managers to take into account realistic uncertainties which affect their pricing analysis.

Let us suppose that the UC Company Ltd is considering the introduction of a new type of soap powder with miracle cleaning properties. A major reason for launching the product at the present time is to provide an alternative to an existing product of similar chemical composition introduced by the PG Company nine months ago.

The UC and PG Companies are the major manufacturers in the soap-powder market and together they account for 90 per cent of the total market for soap powder in the United Kingdom. Both UC and PG have faced considerable criticism in the past from consumers because of the high price of soap powder.

The marketing executives in UC had studied the virtues of the competitive PG product and had come to the conclusion that the late introduction of their miracle powder meant that it was extremely important to establish a sound pricing policy for the new product. Consumer interest in their product would be further aroused if they could show that the UC product was superior in quality to PG's and also available at a competitive price.

UC's executives met to discuss the possible marketing strategies available to them in the light of the fact that *price* would largely be the deciding factor in determining the success of the new-product launch. They felt that they had three initial price alternatives, viz.—set the price at PG's level; raise above PG to establish a quality image; cut the price below PG to try to establish an initial foothold.

The first alternative of meeting PG's price was considered to be the one involving least risk. Because consumers are conditioned to buying PG's miracle powder at its price level, UC's introduction would require the minimum of explanatory advertising about price. Advertising effort could then be concentrated on establishing an image of superior quality and cleaning power over the PG product in order to try to switch PG brand loyal customers to the UC product. In addition pricing at the PG level would be logical because UC would avoid the problem of having to judge either the effect of a high price for UC's product on the consumer or the extent of PG's competitive reaction if UC set the price of miracle powder too low.

Nevertheless, the more adventurous marketing men felt that the late introduction of UC's product necessitated a rather finer price policy. They felt that the accent in marketing the product should be more positive than just trying to catch a proportion of the market share at PG's price. These men felt that an aggressive price-cutting strategy was absolutely necessary and might have the effect of gaining them an initial foothold in the market and as a welcome bonus increasing the overall size of the market at the same time. The size of the market would increase because miracle powder would now be relatively cheaper in relation to other conventional soap-powder brands. Advertising could then be directed both to its cheapness relative to PG's miracle brand and to the improvement in the quality of the "wash" that consumers would get for a relatively small cost if they switched from conventional brands to UC's miracle brand.

Not many of them, however, felt that setting the price of UC's brand above PG's miracle brand would be of much use as a marketing strategy. If price is correlated with quality, and most housewives are motivated by quality considerations in their purchase behaviour, then it may be a defensible strategy. But UC's aim in this situation was to get as much of the market as it possibly could despite the delay in launching miracle powder which had allowed PG to establish a strong market hold. On reflection and discussion none of the decision-makers felt that a "premium" price was a viable alternative strategy and so they decided to concentrate their attention on the "price-equalizing" and "price-cutting" strategies.

The marketing manager decided to analyse these two options in terms of a decision tree. After discussion with his colleagues he felt that the two main chance events which would affect either price policy would be PG's competitive pricing reaction (*raise, stay the same, cut*) and the market-share levels which might occur (*high, medium* or *low*) as a result of the combination of UC's price and PG's price.

The manager drew out the rough decision tree for this situation and this is shown in Table 4.16. For our purposes the marketing manager is assumed to consider only one price-cutting option, namely, cutting the price 10 per cent below PG's existing price.

The marketing manager showed this decision tree to his colleagues and obtained agreement that it was an adequate though simplified description of the complexity of the pricing problem. He then sat down and tried to identify the probability assessments and monetary valuations which he and his fellow decision-makers would have to make. First, for each of UC's two price alternatives an estimate of the probability of PG cutting, raising or maintaining the same price

TABLE 4.16
Rough Decision Tree for UC's Pricing Problem

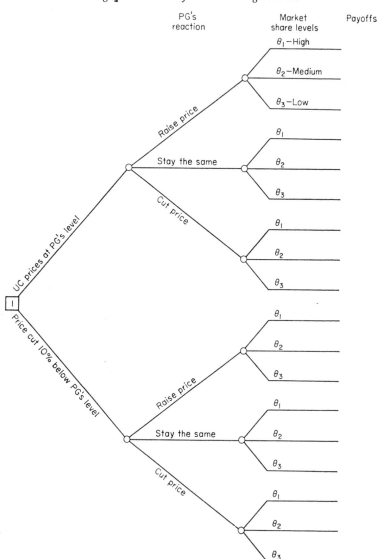

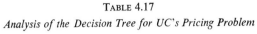

TABLE 4.17

Analysis of the Decision Tree for UC's Pricing Problem

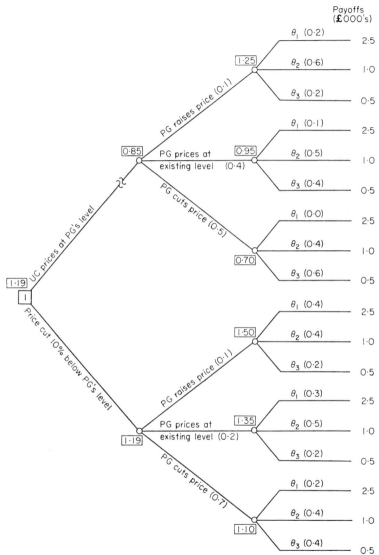

111

TABLE 4.17—(cont.)

Analysis of Decision Point 1   (*Indicates optimal strategy)

Strategy (1)	Chance event (2)	Probability (3)	Payoff (4)	Expected contribution (Col. 3 × Col. 4)
UC prices at PG's Level	PG raises price	0·1	1·25 (Expected payoff)	0·12
	PG prices at existing level	0·4	0·95	0·38
	PG cuts price	0·5	0·7	0·35
			Total	0·85
*UC cuts price by 10%	PG raises price	0·1	1·5	0·15
	PG prices at existing level	0·2	1·35	0·27
	PG cuts price	0·7	1·1	0·77
			Total	1·19

level is required. Similarly, for each combination of UC's price and PG's competitive action, estimates must be provided for UC's likely market share—high (θ_1), medium (θ_2) or low (θ_3)—and the probability of each of these market share levels occurring. In addition, for each market share level the marketing manager has also to estimate the annual contribution to profit net of all operating costs and taxes which would accrue to UC. To do this the marketing manager will probably have to estimate the total market size in terms of number of packets sold or some other suitable unit and by multiplying UC's likely market-share level he can determine UC's market volume.

The decision tree with these monetary and probabilistic assessments is shown in Table 4.17. In addition the alternative pricing policies are analysed in terms of the averaging out and folding back procedure, i.e. the rollback principle.

The analysis shows that price-cutting by 10 per cent increases the expected annual contribution by £0·34 mill. and confirms the marketing men's initial hunch. However, it could be argued that the probability assessments made for the various market share levels are bound to reflect the marketing staff's feelings and it should therefore be no surprise when price-cutting is confirmed as the optimal strategy.

Nevertheless this simple model is useful for evaluating formally a particular price-cutting strategy, i.e. 10 per cent below PG. Alternative 5 per cent, 15 per cent and 20 per cent cuts could also be investigated in terms of this structure. At the same time it should be obvious to the reader that the analysis depends heavily on the ability of the marketing staff to make meaningful estimates of the probabilities of PG's reaction to UC's price and also the *conditional* probabilities of attaining various market share levels given UC's price and PG's competitive price. The monetary valuations of contribution to profit can be made on a much firmer basis because of the involvement of accountants in initially determining the possible price levels on the basis of a markup over the full costs of production, marketing, packaging, etc.

As time goes by and decision-makers have more experience with using decision-tree models, the problems of getting meaningful assessments from decision-makers should become much less difficult. In the meantime major efforts need to be directed towards training decision-makers in these techniques and improving the quality of information systems which exist within firms (so that the decision-maker is provided with all the essential information for analysing any decision problem).

SUMMARY

The case studies have illustrated the following points:

(i) NEW PRODUCT DECISIONS
First, decision analysis provides a framework which indicates how a firm should evaluate the worth of market research and other information-gathering activities such as consumer panels and test markets. Secondly, Bayes' theorem enables the results of a market-research survey (e.g. a test market exercise before a national launch) to be used to revise initial prior probability assessments of the likely sales for a new product.

(ii) OIL AND GAS EXPLORATION DECISIONS
This case discusses whether a wildcatter should gather information through seismographic testing to find out about the prospect's (well's) geological structure before drilling it or push forward and drill without seismic information. If he decides to drill without

information, then his assessments of the chances of getting oil and his valuations of the payoffs from drilling immediately will be based solely on prior information (and thus prior probability assessments). Seismic testing is an information-gathering activity and the information obtained from testing is used to revise the prior probability assessments of getting oil from the particular prospect.

(iii) RESEARCH AND DEVELOPMENT DECISIONS
Research and development projects have to be evaluated before many of the technical and commercial uncertainties are known. The major uncertainty generally confronting the R & D manager is the determination of the likelihood of successfully completing the development work in a given time. If work is not successfully completed within the deadline, the firm can authorize further R & D or abandon the project entirely.

The analysis given is more simplified than it should be in some R & D situations. For example, some R & D managers consciously start work on projects and decide on their viability after carrying out a detailed preliminary phase of R & D work. This preliminary phase can be regarded as information-gathering activity and its effect on project selection can be evaluated using Bayes' theorem as the mechanism for revising prior probabilities about the success of the development work.

(iv) PRICING DECISIONS
This case illustrated the uncertainties involved in establishing a pricing policy for a new product. At the very least, competitive reaction and likely market-share levels are major uncertainties for any marketing director in the determination of a pricing policy. The simple model based on decision-tree concepts showed how the optimal pricing strategy could be evaluated in terms of three possible competitive actions (cut price, raise it or increase it) and three possible market share levels (high, medium and low).

Obviously, simplicity in the model reduces its explanatory power. Yet the value of formal decision analysis in this case should be very clear to the reader.

Finally, all the case studies place considerable value on the use of decision trees as techniques for structuring and understanding the basic elements in a decision problem. It is contended that the solutions obtained from the analysis, through the use of *EMV*, are not necessarily as valuable to the decision-maker as the mental discipline involved in his evaluation of the structure of the problem in terms of the alternatives, chance events, etc., which he *must* consider.

114

References

1. Grayson, C. J., Jr., *Decisions under Uncertainty: Drilling Decisions by Oil and Gas Operators*, Division of Research, Harvard Business School, 1960.
2. Kaufman, G. M., *Statistical Decision and Related Techniques in Oil and Gas Exploration*, Prentice-Hall, 1963.
3. Peck, M., "Science and Technology", in Caves, R. E. *et al.* (eds.), *Britain's Economic Prospects*, Allen and Unwin, 1968.
4. Peck, M., and Scherer, F. M., *The Weapons Acquisition Process*, Division of Research, Harvard Business School, 1962.
5. Meadows, D., "Estimate accuracy and project selection models in industrial research", *Industrial Management Review*, Vol. 8, No. 3, Spring (pp. 105–21).
6. Dean, B. V., *Managerial Economics*, Prentice-Hall, 1953.

PART III

Implementation of Decision-analysis Techniques

5 Using Decision-theory Analysis in Practical Decision Situations

Though decision theory has existed for about two decades, most of the effort has been directed towards theoretical developments of decision-theoretic notions in the field of statistics. Relatively little effort has been channelled towards the application of decision-theory analysis to practical management-decision problems, and, indeed, there is very little evidence to suggest that decision-theory analysis is frequently used in business.

In this chapter we try to explain why decision-analysis methods have not found wide application in industry. We consider first the methodological problems that will have to be resolved before effective applications begin to be widely reported in journals and other media. Second, we will discuss situations in British and U.S. industry to which decision-theory analysis techniques have been applied and suggest situations and business problems in which decision-theory analysis could be applied in order to improve decision-making. Third, we will provide some guidelines for readers who might themselves wish to get started on a decision-analysis exercise in their own firms and hopefully avoid some of the more obvious pitfalls which occur in decision analysis. Finally, we round off with a discussion of the pros and cons of decision analysis and indicate the ways in which the promise of decision-theory analysis can be fulfilled.

The Methodology of Decision Analysis: Issues and Problems

Decision-theory analysis is not one technique but a set of techniques. Alternative methods of decision-theory analysis exist which are not based on the decision-tree concept as such but more on the concept of probability as a state of mind (i.e. subjective probability). We

119

will discuss the most important of these methods in order to put our subsequent discussion of the value of decision-analysis methods into its correct perspective.

Risk analysis, originally suggested by Hertz[1] and Hess and Quigley[2], is a technique which is widely used in management science and O.R. In it the decision-maker has to make subjective probability assessments of the uncertain quantities which are important in a particular decision situation. The technique can most usefully be illustrated in the context of an investment decision. The major problem which a decision-maker has to resolve in an investment decision about, for example, an R & D project, is how much the project is worth in terms of some measure such as net present value (NPV). If the firm knew with certainty the cash-flow pattern which would occur over the project's life-cycle, it would be able to calculate a certain value for NPV. However, uncertainty impinges upon investment decisions and manifests itself in the possibility of unpredicted fluctuations occurring in the cash-flow pattern on the project. The decision-maker, therefore, needs a mechanism which allows him to characterize the effect of uncertainty on the NPV measure. This is best achieved by trying to find the probability distribution of the worth measure so that the *variability* or *spread* about the expected value of NPV can be assessed.

Hertz and Hess and Quigley's method requires that the decision-maker must identify the set of key variables on a project which affect the cash-flow pattern. Once this set is known the risk-analysis method can be applied to give the approximate shape of the probability distribution of NPV.

The steps in the risk-analysis procedure are as follows:

(i) Identify the set of key uncertain factors for the investment decision under consideration (e.g. investment cost, selling price of final product, etc.).

(ii) Obtain estimates of the range of values within which each of these factors will lie and the likelihood of occurrence of each value within the range. For example, price might vary within the range £25–£50 but the decision-maker may, for example, assign probabilities of 0·6 that the price will be £40, of 0·1 that it will be £25, of 0·2 that it will be £45 and of 0·1 that it will be £50.

Often, some of these key factors are interdependent and in these situations we must try to obtain estimates of the correlations between them. These correlations are introduced by means of conditional probability distributions.

(iii) Select by some random procedure a value for each of the key factors from the appropriate probability distributions assessed in Stage (ii). If some of the factors are interdependent, the value obtained from the distribution of one key factor will determine which of several conditional distributions should be sampled to give the value of another key factor.

(iv) This selection process is repeated many times and each time a value for *NPV* is calculated. The distribution of values for *NPV* obtained in this way enables an assessment of the mean value of *NPV* and the variability about the mean value to be given to the decision-maker.

Let us give an example to show how this method works. We assume, first, to avoid introducing the complication of assessing correlation effects between factors that the *net cash flows* in successive years of the project's life are statistically independent and that the economic factors making up the net cash-flow pattern are independently distributed.

The basic economic factors to be considered in our evaluation of an R & D project consist of the following:

(i) development cost per year of the project's life;
(ii) production and sales costs at the point of commercial sale;
(iii) the price at which the product will be sold;
(iv) the quantity which will be sold per year of the project's life.

All the above four factors are estimated in relation to the decision-maker's subjective distribution about the length of the project's life-cycle.

Suppose, for example, that the following estimates are made for an R & D project with an estimated seven-year project life:

(*a*) first-year development cost   mean: £16,000
standard deviation: £1,000

(*b*) second-year development cost   mean: £23,000
standard deviation: £1,000

(*c*) price for years 3 to 7   mean: £800
standard deviation: £50

(*d*) *Quantities sold of final product*
Year 3 mean: 240 units; standard deviation: 24 units

,,	4	,,	275	,,	,,	,,	30	,,
,,	5	,,	280	,,	,,	,,	20	,,
,,	6	,,	250	,,	,,	,,	25	,,
,,	7	,,	200	,,	,,	,,	20	,,

(e) *Production and sales costs in years 3 to 7*

These are assumed to be a proportion of the revenue (price × quantity sold in each year). The assessed proportion is 65 per cent with a standard deviation of 2 per cent.

By means of random selection (we will not consider the exact procedure here though the reader should realize that ERNIE, which picks premium bond winners, is a random-selection machine) the following values could be obtained for each factor:

    (i) Development cost 1st year £15,000
    (ii)   ,,   ,, 2nd year £25,000
    (iii) Price for years 3 to 7   £700
    (iv) Quantities sold 3rd year 220
             ,,   ,, 4th year 280
             ,,   ,, 5th year 260
             ,,   ,, 6th year 250
             ,,   ,, 7th year 200
    (v) Production and sales costs 70 per cent

The net cash flows in each year can then be calculated and are shown in Table 5.1.

TABLE 5.1

Net Cash Flows for R & D Project—One Sample

	Cash Flows	Net Cash Flows (Discounted at 10%)
Year 1 − £15,000	−£15,000	− £15,000
Year 2 − £25,000	−£25,000	− £22,725
Year 3 + 0·3 × (220 × 700)	+£46,200	+ £38,161
Year 4 + 0·3 × (280 × 700)	+£58,800	+ £44,159
Year 5 + 0·3 × (260 × 700)	+£54,600	+ £37,291
Year 6 + 0·3 × (250 × 700)	+£52,500	+ £32,602
Year 7 + 0·3 × (200 × 700)	+£42,000	+ £23,688
		Total = +£138,176 = NPV

The *NPV* obtained for the combination of randomly selected values is +£138,176.

If we selected alternative combinations of values from the distributions we could calculate the net cash flows and *NPV* for each combination. In this way we would obtain several values for *NPV* which would enable us to discover the approximate shape of the distribution for *NPV*. Typical questions that a decision-maker would ask in relation to the *NPV* distribution are:

(i) What is the probability of making a loss (i.e. *NPV* < 0)?

(ii) What is the expected or mean value of *NPV*? (i.e. the value for *NPV* that we would get on average)

(iii) What is the probability of making a gain (i.e. *NPV* > 0)?

(iv) How risky is the project? Is the variability or spread in the *NPV* distribution large in relation to the mean?

In Table 5.2 we present some possible shapes for the *NPV* distribution:

TABLE 5.2

Three Possible Shapes for the NPV Distribution

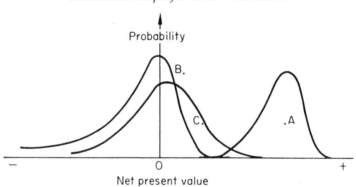

Project C has about a 50/50 chance of getting an *NPV* exceeding zero and is fairly risky. Project A always gives a positive value for *NPV* and there is no probability whatsoever of getting an *NPV* under zero with project A. Project B has about a 90 per cent chance of giving an *NPV* below zero and, therefore, a decision-maker is unlikely to get a positive *NPV* with this project.

In this way it can be seen that knowledge of the shape of the *NPV* distribution can help the decision-maker to assess whether the average or expected *NPV* is likely to give a good indication of the final outcome. However, the exact shape of the *NPV* distribution depends for its validity upon the degree of accuracy with which decision-makers assess subjective probability distributions for the key factors in the decision problem. If these assessments are accurate, the shape of the *NPV* distribution will give a reasonable indication of what might happen if the firm decided to undertake the particular R & D project.

The basic methodology of decision analysis which we have developed in this book is more realistic than the risk-analysis method. This is because the decision-analysis procedure looks at the sequential multi-stage nature of decision-making whereas risk analysis reduces decision-making to a single-stage analysis in which future possible decisions are not considered.

To recapitulate, the essential elements of our decision analysis procedure are:

1 DECOMPOSITION OF THE DECISION PROBLEM IN TERMS OF A DECISION TREE

This decision tree depicts the time-path of the problem in terms of the series of decisions which may have to be made and the chance events which affect those decisions. In operational use the decision tree need only be as complex as the decision itself. If the decision is a simple choice between alternatives then the decision tree in effect is depicting a single-stage rather than the more general multi-stage problem, i.e. the choice between alternatives is made by comparing their respective discounted cash flows. However, the essence of the decision tree is that, no matter how simple or complex the decision problem may be, it forces the decision-maker to define the problem clearly, consider all feasible alternatives and clarify the nature of the risks and uncertainties which he faces. This process of forcing the decision-maker to recognize the structure of his problem in terms of a decision tree can only contribute in the long run to an improvement in the quality of, and rational basis for, decision-making.

2 EVALUATION OF PAYOFF VALUES FOR THE OUTCOMES (OR CONSEQUENCES) IN A DECISION TREE

At this stage we begin to fill in terminal payoff values for the end branches of the skeletal decision tree drawn in Stage I. We assume, as a first approximation, that payoffs should be presented in monetary terms. We also suggest that payoffs should be given in discounted present-value terms using an appropriate internally determined discount rate (or *cost of capital*) for present-value calculations. Where payoff values are unclear (i.e. when you are not prepared to take the accountant's statements at face value!), decision-makers should treat them as uncertain quantities with some probability distribution to be assessed jointly with the financial experts. Any analysis of the tree *could* then be made in terms of the *expected payoff* (or certainty equivalent payoff).

3 THE ASSIGNMENT OF PROBABILITIES AT CHANCE NODES IN A DECISION TREE

Chance events (depicted by circular nodes) affect decision-making at several points of a typical decision tree. The decision-maker must always assign probabilities for these chance events though the task is never easy. Indeed, in many cases these assignments have to be made in terms of subjective probabilities because judgement is the only factor which the decision-maker has at his disposal.

Probability assignments can, in addition, become very difficult when chance events in a decision problem interact with each other. For example, if price and sales are the pivotal uncertain quantities in a marketing decision, the decision-maker's choice of price will affect sales levels. It might be, as is the case for a frequently bought competitive consumer product, that the higher the price, the lower the sales level and vice versa.

4 AVERAGING OUT AND FOLDING BACK—THE ROLLBACK PRINCIPLE

Once the decision tree has been drawn and all probability assignments and payoff values have been evaluated, the decision-maker is in a position to analyse his decision tree. We argued earlier that the rollback concept is the principle by which he should analyse the tree. First, the decision-maker must position himself at the very tips of the tree where the payoff values are given. Second, he must then work backwards through the decision tree by averaging out at each chance-event node in terms of *EMV* and then selecting that path through the tree that yields the maximum *EMV* value at each juncture.

In Chapters 3 and 4 we have given at least five illustrations of the application of rollback principle to the analysis of business decision problems.

Problems: Bushy Mess, Utility, Probability Assessments, Identity of Decision-maker

Nevertheless, despite the obvious logic of the four-step decision-analysis procedure discussed in this book, many problems arise in practice. The most important of these concerns the structure of the tree itself. In most real-life business problems the decision-maker has quite a range of alternatives and uncertainties to consider. If he is not careful the tree can quickly become a "bushy mess" with an overemphasis on the need to take account of every possible eventuality. How should a decision-maker *decompose* the problem, i.e. how should he arrive at a trade-off between the feasibility of the analysis and the need to model reality and complexity as far as possible? There is no simple answer to this question. Effective and meaningful description of a problem in the form of a decision tree really depends upon the decision-maker's ability to see the "wood

for the trees" and concentrate upon the essentials of the problem.
Though decomposition is more art than science, the decision-tree
concept can help to reduce the decision-maker's initial confusion.
If the decision-maker sets out all the possible occurrences and choices
over the planning horizon, he can try out the feasibility of each of
the possible strategies by making rough assessments for probabilities
and payoffs. It may be that certain strategies will turn out to be
clearly dominated by others and in this way several strategy paths
and other branches can be *pruned* out of the tree before a formal
analysis is carried out. Also, by testing the sensitivity of his informal
analysis to changes in his rough assessments of probabilities and
payoffs, he can check again on the feasibility of some of the branches
in the tree.

Though the task of getting a decision tree is a difficult one, decision-
makers tend to draw more realistic trees once they have had sufficient
experience and practice with decision trees. Improvement in the
diagraming of decision trees therefore, will be achieved by
encouraging makers to use them in all their decision problems.

UTILITY VERSUS MONETARY VALUE

Assuming that the skeletal decision flow diagram has been adequately
drawn, a theoretical objection can be made to the description of the
outcomes of paths through the decision tree in terms of money
values. If the decision problem being considered involves large
proportions of the firm's working capital, the attitude of the firm
to the problem may be to avoid risk as far as possible. This would
suggest that money values should be transformed into utility values
and the analysis carried out with these derived utility values. Un-
fortunately the theoretical neatness of the utility concept has not
been matched by acceptance of its merit by practising decision-
makers. Grayson's[3] oil and gas wildcatters were sceptical about
utility and this finding has been replicated in several other studies,
e.g. Thomas[4], Green[5]. Equally, there can be no doubt that decision-
makers on the whole tend to be risk-averse (see Swalm[6]) because
organizational structures in firms tend to reward steady rather than
spectacular performance.

Some firms, notably McKinsey (see Hespos and Strassmann),[7]
use a simulation approach with decision trees to allow for risk-
aversion situations. Since decision-makers are not willing to act
on the basis of *EMV* (but do not accept utility either!) they suggest
that for each possible strategy on the decision tree the monetary
implications can be obtained in terms of a probability distribution
on the payoff (*NPV*), i.e. a payoff density curve can be obtained for
each strategy. The means and variances of these curves are calculated

and the curves are compared one with the other. Strategies whose *NPV* curves are everywhere of lower value than others are eliminated immediately. The strategies that remain must really be evaluated by obtaining the decision-maker's utility-for-money curve. However, in practice, many firms look upon *variance* of the *NPV* as a measure of risk and ask the decision-makers to trade off mean against variance informally in coming to a decision. For example, a large firm may only want a positive value for *NPV*. Operationally, this means that the decision-maker must hope to find that the probability of $NPV < 0$ is acceptably low.

Nevertheless even with this "simulation of decision tree" (or *stochastic* decision tree) approach, the decision-maker cannot really get away from making a utility assessment. The only sensible solution for him is to obtain the utility-for-money curve and analyse the decision tree in terms of expected utility values.

It is clear that a great deal of work will be done in the next few years to make the utility concept more operationally meaningful to decision-makers. One very promising direction is to view utility as a multi-dimensional function of several possible attributes, e.g. money value, market share, etc. The aim would then be to describe the outcomes in terms of these multi-attributed utilities. For example, in an R & D situation, the decision to invest in a project might not solely be based on the likely rate of return. Other factors such as the *time* necessary for the completion of development work and the *costs of development* may be valid alternative project attributes.

Utility assessment procedures will clearly improve and so we can still accept the relevance of *EUV* (expected utility value) or *EMV* (expected monetary value, if we are indifferent to risk) as the criteria by which we determine the optimal alternative in a decision analysis.

WHO IS THE DECISION-MAKER?

However, the whole of decision analysis is based upon the concept of the individual decision-maker. This "individual" is either some single manager to whom a measure of authority for decision-making has been delegated by the firm or a group with a similar set of delegated responsibilities. The objectives of this single individual or group may differ quite considerably from those of the firm. This raises the issue of whether we should regard the firm as the true decision-maker and try to analyse decisions from the firm's viewpoint. At present, the answer to this question must be "No!" since the group or "individual" is charged with responsibility for decision-making. In the longer term, however, we should expect theoreticians to try to develop operational procedures for carrying out decisions in terms of the firm's stated set of objectives. This would involve the determination of a relevant utility function for the firm as a whole.

The most difficult problem in decision analysis is the process of assessing probabilities. Decision-makers are called upon to assess probabilities for single uncertain quantities as well as to make joint assessments for several uncertain quantities. In addition, some of these uncertain quantities are correlated, which means that several conditional probability assessments will also have to be made.

In practice, the decision-maker must sit down and decide, first, how many quantities really *are* uncertain. Once he has done this, the assessment procedure really involves him in processing objective data for each uncertain quantity into meaningful subjective assessments. All the evidence (see Winkler[8], for example) suggests that there is no way of ensuring that satisfactory probability assessments are obtained. Different decision-makers give different assessments for the same uncertain quantity and this reflects the different frames of reference which they have when processing the available information.

In the long run, decision-makers' experience with probability assessments may improve their quality. At present, a lot of the subjective probability data in decision analyses are "soft" numbers and great reliance cannot yet be placed on the results of those cases in which decisions are made solely on prior information (i.e. before any option to collect further information is exercised).

A great deal of research work is obviously needed in the area of subjective probability. Questions such as "How much objective information about the decision problem should be given to the decision-maker?" and "How much training about probability concepts should be given to the decision-maker?" need to be answered. Issues concerning the best methods to use when assessing subjective probabilities for dependent uncertain quantities need to be resolved.

Pros and Cons of Decision Analysis

At this stage it is useful to question whether decision-analysis techniques should be used in practical analyses of decision problems. The main arguments for and against these techniques are presented in the following table.

Pro	Con
1 Systematic and logical approach to decision-making	1 Time consuming
2 Helps communication within the firm—experts in other areas are consulted in decision-making	2 Lack of acceptance by all decision-makers
3 Permits a thorough analysis of alternative options	3 Assessments of probabilities and utilities are difficult to obtain
4 Separation of utility assessment (preference assessment for outcomes) from probability assessments for uncertain quantities	4 Evaluates the decision in "soft" number terms because input data at present are "soft"
5 Allows decision-maker to judge how much information to gather in a given decision problem	

All the brief summary above really says is that you must balance the newness of the technique against admitted measurement problems. If you are able to accept the step-by-step logic of the procedure then you should join the increasing band of decision-makers applying decision theory to real problems.

Usefulness of Decision Analysis

One question that business executives always ask in the discussion after lectures on decision analysis is "where have these techniques been applied successfully?" The list of applications is ever growing and reference should be made to Brown[9] for an up-to-date report of American applications.

Areas in which decision analysis techniques have been successfully applied are:

    (i) investment decisions—new plant, etc;
    (ii) new product decisions;
    (iii) sales force decisions;
    (iv) market research decisions;
    (v) research and development decisions;
    (vi) oil and gas exploration decisions;
    (vii) pricing decisions;
   (viii) competitive bidding decisions;
    (ix) quality control decisions;
    (x) machine set-up problems in production.

Areas to which these techniques could be applied are limitless. I would speculate that routine decisions about such diverse things as medical diagnoses and macro-economic policies and decisions by governments will be made in the near future using decision-analysis techniques as guidelines for decisions. The future is bright and rewarding for any decision-maker who wants to make rational decisions and use a rational decision-analysis framework for doing so.

Getting Started on a Decision Analysis

For those readers who feel they would like to try a decision analysis themselves in their own firms, the following guidelines about getting started are suggested:

1 Make sure that you get your colleagues enthusiastic about and interested in decision analysis. Make sure that your superiors and other colleagues see the value of, and payoff to be obtained from, decision analysis.

2 Having done this, make sure that you define the decision problem correctly, i.e. check that you are analysing the correct problem.

3 Try several alternative decompositions and decision trees for the problem before going through the assessment process. It is often useful to hire the services of a decision analyst for your first decision analysis. He has done so many that he can guide you and also discuss problem structure as a non-involved third party.

4 Before getting probability assessments from decision-makers, you must make sure that they are fully trained in the concepts and meaning of probability. This training is best done by a staff member, who is competent at probability, giving a series of informal lectures in the context of the firm.

5 When decision-makers have to assign probabilities for some uncertain quantity, e.g. *price*, you must give those decision-makers all the objective, quantitative information about price levels which is available in the firm (e.g. from accounting records, past sales data, etc.).

6 Stick to *EMV* on your first analysis. Bring in the utility concept gradually and remember how to assess an utility-for-money function (see Mr Z's decision problem in Chapter 3). Consult with a decision analyst if you find the utility concept difficult to implement.

Finally, the best possible note on which to conclude is to wish the reader good luck with the implementation exercise if he gets round to doing it. If he does, and he is successful, then this book will have achieved its purpose.

References

1. Hertz, D. B., "Risk Analysis in Capital Investment", *Harvard Business Review*, 1964.
2. Hess, S. W., and Quigley, H. A., "Analysis of Risk in Investments using Monte Carlo Techniques", *Chemical Engineering Symposium Series* 42: *Statistics and Numerical Methods in Chemical Engineering*, New York, American Institute of Chemical Engineering, 1963, p. 55.
3. Grayson, C. J., Jr., *Decisions Under Uncertainty: Drilling Decisions by Oil and Gas Operators*, Division of Research, Harvard, 1960.
4. Thomas, H., Econometric and Decision Analysis Studies in R & D, (Unpublished Ph.D. thesis, Edinburgh, 1970).
5. Green, P. E., "Risk Attitudes and Chemical Investment Decisions", *Chemical Engineering Progress*, January 1963.
6. Swalm, R. O. "Utility Theory", *Harvard Business Review*, 1965.
7. Hespos, R. F., and Strassmann, P. A., "Analysis of Investment Decisions", *Management Science*, 1965.
8. Winkler, R. L., "The Assessment of Prior Distributions in Bayesian Analysis", *Journal Amer. Statist. Ass.*, 62, 1967, pp. 776–95.
9. Brown, R. V., "Do managers find decision theory useful?", *Harvard Business Review*, May–June 1970, pp. 78–90.

Annotated Reading List

The major contributions in the area of decision theory have come from the group working at Harvard Business School under Professors Howard Raiffa and Robert O. Schlaifer.

Two of their books, viz. *Applied Statistical Decision Theory* by H. Raiffa and R. O. Schlaifer (Harvard, 1961) and *Introduction to Statistical Decision Theory* by J. W. Pratt, H. Raiffa and R. O. Schlaifer (McGraw-Hill preliminary edition 1965), are at a mathematical level and recommended for readers who wish to delve into statistical decision theory and, particularly, problems of statistical inference. However, most of the conceptual ground that is necessary is covered in two excellent practical decision-analysis manuals, one by Schlaifer and the other by Raiffa. Schlaifer's *Analysis of Decisions under Uncertainty* (McGraw-Hill, 1967) was written as the text for the core Harvard MBA course in decision theory. It is an excellent practical guide for the manager who wants to carry out a decision analysis and contains numerous examples and cases which can be attempted as the text progresses. Raiffa's *Decision Analysis* (Addison-Wesley, 1968) is a classic because it captures the flavour of decision analysis in an extremely palatable expository form. The logic of the methods of decision analysis and the conceptual problems which have to be faced in implementing decision-analysis techniques are the main points of emphasis of this text.

Recently, three texts have appeared from British authors which present the theory of decision-making in different ways. Aitchison's *Choice against Chance* (Addison-Wesley, 1971) is an excellent text on statistical decision theory which reduces the mathematical argument to a minimum and concentrates upon the logic of decision-theory analysis. Lindley's *Making Decisions* (Wiley, 1970) is aimed at much the same market as Raiffa's but covers a narrower field in an excellent statistical exposition. Moore's *Risk in Business Decision* (Longmans, London Business School series) is the text which has been written for the core statistical decision-making course on the MSc programme. It covers the essential points of the texts on Bayesian statistics and formal decision analysis and is well written with numerous examples.

The following seems to be a minimum reading list of articles in the area:

Howard, R. A., "Decision Analysis: Applied Decision Theory", *Proceedings IFORS Conference*, Boston, 1966.

Magee, J. F., "Decision Trees for Decision-making", *Harvard Business Review*, Vol. 42, No. 4, 1964, pp. 126–38.

Magee, J. F., "How to Use Decision Trees in Capital Investment", *Harvard Business Review*, Vol. 42, No. 5, 1964, pp. 79–96.

Green, P. E., "Bayesian Decision Theory in Pricing Strategy", *Journal of Marketing*, 1963.

Moore, P. G., and Thomas, H., "How to Measure Your Risk"—Pethow Company" and "A Tree to Tease Your Mind—Pethow Company", *Financial Times*, 18 and 19 January 1972.

Swalm, R. O., "Utility Theory—Insights into Risk Taking", *Harvard Business Review*, 1965.

Hammond III, J. S., "Better Decisions through Preference Theory", *Harvard Business Review*, 1967.

Winkler, R. L., "The Assessment of Subjective Probability Distributions in Bayesian Analysis", *Journal of the American Statistical Association*, 1967, Vol. 62, pp. 776–95.

Winkler, R. L., "The Quantification of Judgement: Some Methodological Suggestions", *Journal of the American Statistical Association*, 1967, Vol. 62, pp. 1105–20.

Winkler, R. L., "*The Consensus of Subjective Probability Estimates*", *Management Science*, Vol. 15, No. 2, Series B, pp. 61–75.

Moore, P. G., and Thomas, H., "Measurement Problems in Decision Analysis", *London Business School Working Paper*, 1972.

Index

b after a page reference indicates bibliographical reference

135

Expected value, 20, 30
  of perfect information, 89
  of sample (test market) information, 90, 92

FOOD products, uncertain quantities in, 24

GAMBLING decisions, 33, 34, 38–9
Gas exploration decisions, 94–9, 113–4
Graphs (histograms), 18, 19
Grayson, C. J., Jr., 66, 75b, 94, 115b, 126, 131b
Green, P. E., 126, 131b

HARVARD Business School, 21, 94
Hertz, D. B., 120, 131b
Hespos, R. F., 126, 131b
Hess, S. W., 120, 131b
Histograms, 18, 19
Hurwicz, L., 36, 37, 42b, 73

INSTANT potato, launching, 80–88
Investment-analysis techniques, 43
Investment-appraisal formulae, 43–4
Investment decisions, 4–5, 24, 43, 47–58, 101

KAUFMAN, G. M., 94, 115b

LONDON Airport, siting, 63

McKINSEY & Company, 126
Market research, 9
  survey information, valuation of, 88–94
Maximax, 36
Maximin, 35–6, 64
Meadows, D., 100, 115b
Merrett, A. J., 61, 75b
Minimax, 73
Mixed strategies, 36
Modal level, 20
Monetary value v. utility, 126–7
Moroney, M. J., 21, 30b
Multiplication rule for probabilities, 13–16

NPV, 120–4
Net gain from sample information, 94
Net present value (NPV), 120–4
New product decisions, 8, 9, 24, 27, 32, 34, 80–94, 113

OBJECTIVES, 32–3
Oil exploration decisions, 94–9, 113–14
Once-and-for-all decisions, 5
Operational research, 120
Opportunity loss criterion, 36–8
Optimal strategy, evaluation of, 52–8
Optimism, 36

PAYOFF matrix, 41
Payoffs (value measures), 32–4, 47–8, 50–1, 75, 124
Peck, M., 100, 115b
Pessimism (Maximin), 35–6, 64
Postponement strategy, 28
Pratt, J. W., 21
Pricing decisions, 107–13, 114
Probabilities—
  assignment of, 128
  estimation of, 75
  revision of, 66–71
Probability—
  and uncertainty, 10
  density function, 28
  distributions, 18–21, 28–9
  measurement of, 6–10
  rules of, 16–18
  subjective, 8–9, 24–6
  theory, 3–30
  tree diagrams, 11, 15, 16, 17, 29

QUIGLEY, H. A., 120, 131b

RAIFFA, H., 21, 26, 30b, 46, 75b
Regret criterion, 36–8
Relative frequency, 7–8
Research and development decisions, 5–6, 27–8, 100–7, 114, 120–4
Risk analysis, 120–4
Risk problems, 34
Rollback principle, 53, 54, 56, 67, 70, 74, 125

SAVAGE, L. J., 36, 42b
Scherer, F. M., 109, 115b
Schlaifer, R. O., 21
Scott, W. P., 75b
Simulation of decision tree, 127
Single-stage decisions, 44
Soap powder, pricing, 108–13
Standard deviation, 20, 30
States of nature, 32–4
Stochastic decision tree, 127
Stokes (Donald), *Lord*, 17